40

DAYS TO FREEDOM

DISCOVERING HOW TO LIVE THE NEW LIFE GOD HAS PROVIDED

MATT MUSCATELL

40 Days to Freedom: Discovering How to Live in the New Life God Has Provided
Copyright 2019 by Matthew Muscatell

ISBN: 978-1-7343312-0-2 (Print)

978-1-7343312-1-9 (Digital)

Printed in the USA.

Though it may seem I am stating the obvious,
I dedicate my first book to the One who loved
me first and gave His life for my freedom:
Jesus Christ.

CONTENTS

FOREWORD

L iving things grow. Whether we are talking about a potted plant, a baby seal, or a human infant, a defining characteristic of all living things is that they are designed to develop over time. While this may seem obvious, it is not automatic. Growth does not just occur on its own. Healthy growth requires an environment with two things: food and exercise. We need both energy and action in order to thrive.

Spiritual growth is no different. In order to experience real personal development in our character, minds, and spirit we must be intentional. We must feed our hearts and minds on the right nutrients and then take the right actions to develop robust and effective spiritual lives.

In this book, Matt Muscatell has assembled a forty-day package of powerful growth-enhancing spiritual nutrients and daily exercises. It is designed for your growth. Every reading is packed with powerful truths from God's Word and daily exercises designed to stimulate your spiritual development.

Pick it up every day. Read and take action. You will grow—you will thrive! You are only forty days away from a better version of your life.

— John Carter
Founder and Lead Pastor
Abundant Life Christian Center, Syracuse, NY

PROLOGUE

Life seemed to get away from him. As he stared off into the prison cell, he wondered why he had become the person who led him to this point. He thought of his upbringing and the people who helped shape him. He reviewed the feelings of rejection, anger, and frustration that he felt throughout his life. The choices he made certainly didn't help his current state. Battling addictions, choices led by deep hurts that were not addressed, and negative information were all a part of false thinking that made him who he was. "I am locked and bound in this cell, but my whole life has been a prison. I am not only bound on the outside, but I have been enslaved on the inside."

As the shackles on his hands and feet served as a constant reminder of his hopeless condition, he noticed a bright reflection every time he moved his head a certain way. *Was he imagining?* "Could it be true?" he wondered, "How could this be*?"* As he redirected his focus, he saw the way to freedom! This man, bound in shackles and locked in prison, began to rise up with hope because he saw keys. Though he was bound, the keys were the answer to unlocking himself from the chains and the prison doors. This was great news!

As he picked up the keys, he noticed engraving on them. The engraving said, "You are free to go. The price has been paid."

He thought to himself, "Is this real? It seems too easy. Could this be a trick? I'm not sure if I can believe this. I don't deserve to be free. I should pay for my wrongdoing. This is my fault and need to conquer this on my own."

The man enslaved in his prison reasoned within himself again. He began to think, "I wonder what it feels like to actually be free! Maybe

I should take these keys and walk in freedom. Will people see me differently? Will they believe me? Do I really want to be free? I know I need help. I'm at rock bottom." Then he spoke to himself out loud, "Yes, I'm sick of being bound and shackled.

As this man sat in his prison, he knew he needed to make a choice. Indecision would keep him in the same old condition. A decision to apply the keys to his shackles would set him free. What is this man going to do?

INTRODUCTION

For we were slaves. Yet our God did not forsake us in
our bondage; but He extended mercy to us...to revive us
(Ezra 9:9).

H umanity needs to be free. Many people suffer day by day, moment
by moment, bound and in prison. No, I'm not necessarily talking
about those who have committed crimes and are in a physical
prison, though it does include those who are presently in that state. What
I'm talking about are those circumstances, habits, and ways of life that
keep people far from enjoying all that God created them to be.

Maybe you picked up this book and said, "Yes, there are areas of my
life where I need to be free." Perhaps today you are not free emotionally,
but enslaved by the torment of fear, anxiety, rejection, loneliness,
depression, discouragement, or hurt in the deep places of your heart. You
may be battling physical bondage through sickness and other ailments that
keep you from wholeness and great health. Spiritually, you are addicted
to some sort of sin. You fight, but fall. Then you get up and fight, but fall
again. Jealousy, envy, unforgiveness, cursing, lust, greed, and dishonoring
others may be part of your list of struggles.

The book of Exodus speaks about the children of Israel being slaves
in bondage to Egypt. Exodus 1:13-14 says that the Egyptians caused the
"children of Israel [to] serve with harshness" (Darby) and that they made
the Israelite's lives bitter because of the hard bondage.

This is how the enemy, Satan, works in your life. His desire is to
deceive you so you will suffer the consequences of bondage. John 10:10
says, "The thief does not come except to steal, and to kill, and to destroy."

The will of the devil is to make you enslaved and stuck in the chains of bondage, far from experiencing freedom. And much like the Egyptians made life harsh for the children of Israel in the book of Exodus, Satan desires to see you bitter, depressed, hurt, without purpose, and ineffective as you experience spiritual, mental, emotional, and physical bondage.

The good news today is that God hears your heart's cry to be free. He loves you and is full of tender mercies toward you. Exodus 2:23-25 says, "Then the children of Israel groaned because of the bondage, and they cried out; and their cry came up to God because of the bondage. So God heard their groaning…And God looked upon the children of Israel, and God acknowledged them."

> The good news today is that God hears your heart's cry to be free. He loves you and is full of tender mercies toward you.

God is love, and He never hears our cry without action. God is not a passive, uncaring God. God responds with an answer to our bondage in order to set us free. In Exodus 3 we see God calling a man named Moses to be an instrument in His hands to set the children of Israel free. Moses was the voice of God to declare the heart and purpose of God for the children of Israel. Exodus 5:1 says, "Thus says the Lord God of Israel: 'Let My people go.'"

God desires for all men and women to be free from the bondage that entangles them. His declaration of "Let my people go!" permeates the Word of God, especially in Jesus Christ. John 10:10 continues by saying, "I have come that they may have life, and that they may have it more abundantly." Jesus came to make you and I free and to experience abundant life in every area of our lives. Jesus is life and freedom in your body. Jesus is life and freedom in your mind and emotions. Jesus is new life and freedom in your spirit. Jesus frees your body, soul, and spirit!

In fact, freedom is why Jesus came. In Luke 4:18-19, Jesus declares His mission of love and freedom to all of humanity:

The Spirit of the Lord is upon Me, because He has anointed Me to preach the gospel to the poor, He has sent me to heal the brokenhearted, to proclaim liberty to the captives and recovery of sight to the blind, to set at liberty those who are oppressed; to proclaim the acceptable year of the Lord.

Do you see that? Jesus came to set people free. Jesus came to set you free. He came for those in need; the brokenhearted, the captives, the blind, and the oppressed. Jesus offers the gospel, or good news, that saves, heals, and brings freedom.

WHERE TO BEGIN

You may be asking, "Where do I begin? Where does freedom start?"

Freedom is not defined as doing whatever we want. There are many who can attest to the fact that they did what they wanted and paid the consequences.

Freedom is defined as doing what God desires. God created us to be free, so His way leads to life and blessing (Deuteronomy 30:19).

The problem we face as humans is that none of us have fully done what God desires. The Bible calls this sin. Sin literally means that we miss the mark. In other words, we have not, do not, and cannot live holy, perfect lives. We miss the mark of holiness; we fall short. Romans 3:23 says, "All have sinned and fall short of the glory of God," and elsewhere it says, "there is none righteous" (Romans 3:10).

Jesus says that all who have sinned have become a slave of sin (John 8:34). Our nature is to disobey God, and our disobedience results in death (Romans 6:23). However, God has delivered us from destruction (Psalm 107:20). All that we experience on this earth that is negative is the consequences of our disobedience to God's Word, plan, and perfect will. So when we are enslaved to sin we are empty, we struggle, we experience pain, we get addicted, we are in a constant battle against emotional bondage, physical pain, mental torment, and spiritual decay.

The good news is that Christ Jesus loves you and did not come to condemn you, but save you, deliver you, heal you, restore you, and set you free. He did this by taking your sin on Himself on the cross, becoming the curse of sin, and thus destroying the chains of sin's penalty and power.

Freedom begins in your life today by accepting God's forgiveness and receiving Jesus by faith. It starts by recognizing that you have sinned against God, but realizing that God loves you so much to free you and transform you. You cannot earn salvation or a relationship with Jesus. Ephesians 2:8 says that you are saved by grace, not by works, but through faith.

Freedom begins in your life today by accepting God's forgiveness and receiving Jesus by faith.

When you accept Jesus as your Lord and Savior, trusting fully in Him, knowing that His death and resurrection was for you, you become a new creation, the old things have passed away and the new things have come (2 Corinthians. 5:17 NASB). You are no longer a slave, but a son or daughter of God who has been set free! (See John 1:12 and 8:35.)

Today can be the start to your freedom by accepting and knowing Jesus personally. Spiritual, emotional, and physical freedom starts now as you accept Him.

Pray this prayer from your heart, not as a religious practice, but be genuine and authentic with God. Let this prayer guide you as you talk from your heart to God to receive Christ. Freedom begins today!

Lord Jesus, I come to You today confessing that I am a sinner. I have sinned against You and realize that I have disobeyed You. I am sorry and want to change. I believe that You love me so much that You died on the cross for my sins and paid the penalty for me. I believe that You rose from the dead and have defeated the power of sin and death. Forgive me. I trust fully in the work of the cross and right now accept You by faith. Save me Jesus. I receive You into my life as my Lord and Savior.

Thank You for setting me free today. Thank You that starting today, I now have a relationship with You! Thank You that I am new and can start a new life by being born again! Amen.

If you accepted Jesus Christ by praying that prayer, you are now born again! In 2 Corinthians 5:17 Paul states that you are now a new creation, the old has passed, the new has begun! Freedom has started in your life because you are now in Christ, and Christ is in you!

HOW TO GET THE MOST OUT OF THE NEXT FORTY DAYS

The purpose of this book is to be a tool that gives you principles of freedom that are not new, yet if followed wholly, will make you new. These principles are not mine, nor are they invented by mankind. The principles and promises found in this devotional are God's, found in the Bible, or the Word of God. These principles work when received by faith and applied to one's everyday life.

I encourage you to stick with it on a daily basis. Use this devotional as a way in which you dig deeper in God's Word, spend quality time with Jesus, and allow Him to do a wonderful work in you.

Don't rush through. Set a time each day, and, if needed, schedule this time with God. Remember, you will benefit greatly and receive so much in God's presence when you value time with Him and make it a priority in your daily routine.

There are forty chapters, divided into eight topics. Each topic includes five days of devotionals. Each topic is an anchor point that will destroy the enemy's lies and weapons that have brought torment and destructive patterns into your life.

Each day's devotional is followed by an application of Worship, Prayer, Declaration, and Action. James 1:22 says, "But be doers of the word, and not hearers only, deceiving yourselves." It is important to understand that taking this book out and learning about God's Word and way to freedom is so important, but if you do not act on God's Word, it will have no effect on your life. God not only desires that you gain *information*, but by receiving and acting on what He says, you will experience *transformation*.

God has good plans for you (Jeremiah 29:11). No matter how you feel, based on what you've done or what you are in the midst of dealing with today, God loves you and is for you. He went to great lengths to provide for your freedom. He has come to set you free.

I believe that in the days ahead, wicked desires, bad habits, spiritual chains, and stubborn strongholds will be crushed by the Spirit of the Lord. Your breakthrough and victory are at hand. In fact, Jesus said, "It is finished" (John 19:30).

Freedom has been secured for you!

It's my prayer that within the following pages you experience all that God desires for you, and that you become transformed in the presence of God.

WHY FORTY DAYS?

The Word of God uses numbers to represent something that God wants to communicate and "drive home" in the hearts of people. One of the numbers that is seen throughout the Bible, both in the Old Testament and the New Testament, is the number forty. This is a significant number and is important to understand as you begin this forty-day devotional.

The number forty is used by God as a number associated with testing, trial, and preparation. You may look at this meaning and be tempted to become discouraged at first, but the testing that is used by God is an extremely positive work that He does, as long as you are willing to surrender and cooperate.

There is a cycle that is used during the forty days of testing. The *testing* is preparation in your life. The testing comes to prepare you for a *transition*. God is not interested in keeping you in the testing period, nor does He take pleasure in doing it. The purpose is to prepare you for a *transition*, or a change. Once the testing period is finished and you take a step into the transition God desired, there is *transformation*. You are changed for good and God receives great glory. The purpose of testing and trial is not to break you, but to transition you to a new beginning, a resurrection, and transformation.

The purpose of testing and trial is not to break you, but to transition you to a new beginning, a resurrection, and transformation.

During the days of Noah rain fell for forty days and forty nights. From this came a new beginning and transformation on the earth (Genesis 7:4). Moses spent time in God's presence on the mountain for forty days and forty nights, and the Ten Commandments were written on tablets (Exodus 34:28). Israel wandered for forty years in the wilderness, and then finally experienced a new beginning and transformation by entering the Promised Land (Numbers 14:33-34; Joshua 3:14-17). After Goliath tested and taunted Israel for forty days, a transformation came when David slew him and God delivered Israel from the hand of their enemies (1 Samuel 17). Jesus fasted forty days and forty nights before He was tempted by the devil. Once Jesus overcame His testing period, He was thrust into full-time ministry with anointing and power (Matthew 4:2, 17). Even after Jesus rose from the dead, He remained on the earth for forty days before His transformation that came from ascending to heaven (Acts 1:3).

The number forty: *testing, transition, and transformation.* During the next forty days, you will be tested and tempted. How do I know that? Because the devil does not want you free. He does not want you prepared to be transitioned to freedom from bondage. The good news is that God does. It is the will of God for you to be free because He already provided for your freedom.

Be encouraged that God is for you and not against you. He will empower you to continue this devotional, be a disciple in His Word, and to practice all that you learn. You will see and experience wonderful freedom and transformation after these forty days—and for years to come!

PART 1: READ

Abide in the Word of God

DAY 1: WHAT IS THE WORD OF GOD?

"I rejoice at Your word as one who finds great treasure"
(Psalm 119:162).

The first step to your road to victory, or to experiencing true freedom in your life, is to read the Word of God. The Bible is not an old, lifeless book that has no relevance for today. In fact, God's Word is exactly that: words spoken by God. Since they are God's words, they have power, life, and all that you need.

David said, "I rejoice at Your word as one who finds great treasure." That certainly sums up God's Word. It is great treasure because it reveals who God is, what He has done, what He does today, and what He will do in the future. God's Word is full of principles and promises that you can trust in. Why trust in God's Word? Well, a word that is spoken will only go as far as one's nature and character. God's nature is holy; His character is flawless. So whatever God says is trustworthy because who He is and what He does stands behind the word.

God's Word is His will and purpose, His heart and mind. You discover the plans of God and the purposes of God in your own life as you read the Word. Since God's Word reveals His heart and shows how He thinks and acts, you can get to know God on a personal level. Your ongoing relationship with God can grow by reading God's Word. Knowing God and growing closer to Christ is possible through His Word.

Jesus said, "If you abide in My word, you are My disciples indeed" (John 8:31). One of the signs that you are a disciple of Jesus is that you abide in God's Word. The Greek word for *abide* that is used in this passage is *meno*. It literally means, "To continue, remain, to dwell, rest, lodge, to settle, stay." To abide in the Word of God means that you remain constant in it. You live in the Word because you know that the Word of God gives you life and you experience true freedom. To abide in the Word of God means that you dwell in it and allow it to dwell in you richly (Colossians 3:16). Abiding in God's Word is resting, depending, and surrendering to the treasure that is freely given.

> God's Word is His will and purpose, His heart and mind. You discover the plans of God and the purposes of God in your own life as you read the Word.

God has much treasure for you to experience. The question is, have you picked up God's Word to read it? Are you abiding, remaining, and resting in God's words that give life? Whatever you need freedom from, the Bible has the answer. As you abide in the Word, eternal treasure is yours and you will never be the same again!

APPLICATION

WORSHIP:
Sit before the Lord and worship Him for His perfect Word that is full of treasure and life for you today! Take time and sing to God, thanking Him that you can trust in Him and in what He says, every time.

PRAYER:
"Lord Jesus, I long to know You by knowing your Word. I renew my commitment to read Your Word so that I don't miss the treasure of knowing You and receiving all that You have provided for my life. I rest, remain, and make my home in Your Word. I am amazed that as I abide in Your Word, that the truth of Your Word abides in me. I receive Your Word, in Jesus' name. Amen."

DECLARATION:

"I declare out loud today that I rejoice at the Word of God, for in it God declares His treasure of life and freedom over my life!"

ACTION:

Take steps to read the Bible more. If you haven't ever read the Word of God, just start by setting aside fifteen minutes a day to read it. When you know the value of what God has in store for you, it will motivate you to read it more than anything else. God has much to say, and whatever He says, you can trust. Guard and schedule this time daily as you read this devotional. God will do more in you and through you than you can ever imagine!

DAY 2: WHAT DOES THE WORD OF GOD DO?

For the word of God *is* living and powerful, and sharper than any two-edged sword, piercing even to the division of soul and spirit, and of joints and marrow, and is a discerner of the thoughts and intents of the heart (Hebrews 4:12).

Yesterday we took a look at what God's Word is; it is truth and treasure for you. You may ask, "I understand what the Word of God is, but what does reading God's Word do for me?" You may seek further understanding. Maybe you are asking, "I see that it gives me life and freedom since it's God's promises and principles I can trust in, but how do I benefit specifically?"

The reason that God's Word is vital for your growth in the Lord as well as your freedom is because God's Word is living and powerful! It isn't just a historical book for learning facts about God, but it is also a book that produces life in every area of your life. The Word of God is full of His life and His power, and the benefits that come with attending to His words and keeping them in your heart is life and healing! (Proverbs 4:20-22).

God's Word is a lamp that sheds light on your circumstances and directs you in the way that you should go (Psalm 119:105). This has proven to be true so many times in my life, but one instance particularly stands out. I was seeking the Lord for guidance and direction; I needed to know His will before making a major decision. As I spent time with Him in the early morning hour, I was reading His Word and was also being ministered to by Charles Spurgeon's devotional, *Morning and Evening*.

On this particular day, there was a passage of scripture that went with the devotional that spoke to me. The Holy Spirit gripped my heart and spoke so powerfully to me as to what I should do. He used the devotional to lead me to the scripture passage, which guided me and led me. What was even greater than getting direction was the fact that I sensed the presence of God so strong with me at that moment. I not only knew that God was with me, but felt such freedom, power, and overwhelming love. I was truly amazed and awestruck, not wanting to leave the room where God was ministering to me and speaking to me. God's Word and His presence led me, and I was able to know Him and experience the beauty and majesty of His presence.

The Word of God empowers you to live pure and holy before God (Psalm 119:9-11). It has creative power and makes a way where there is no way (Genesis 1:3; Romans 4:17). Studying the Bible will build your faith and encourage you to believe what God says (Romans 10:17; Acts 20:32).

Studying the Bible will build your faith and encourage you to believe what God says.

When you abide in God's Word, His words will comfort you during affliction (Psalm 119:50). Taking time in God's Word brings wonderful freedom (John 8:31-32). When God's Word becomes your life day and night, it will abide in you and you will find great success and prosperity (Joshua 1:8). You will gain wisdom from an all-wise God (Proverbs 2:1-7; 4:5). The words that God speaks to you as you read the Bible will penetrate the dark clouds of depression and despair, and will fill you great joy! (John 15:11). The peace of God will fill your life, no matter what season of life you are in for He has overcome the world (John 16:33). God's Word heals your body and soul (Psalm 107:20).

As we walk through life, we need to be warned of things, especially when we cannot see clearly up ahead. God's Word warns us and protects us (Psalm 19:9-11). His Word convicts us of sin and shows us the times we disobey Him (Titus 1:9). The living and powerful Word of God fills you with power and strength to live in freedom and victory (1 John 2:14).

Since God is eternal and is infinite, all that He promises through His Word is more than you can ever imagine. These promises of blessings that come through the living and powerful Word of God is yours, but you need to start by reading and abiding in it. It is a seed that is sown (Mark 4:14), and it will bless you abundantly, but the words that are sown in your life from reading and abiding in it will only produce good fruit on good ground (Mark 4:20).

By keeping your heart open and soft toward God's Word, you will benefit greatly from what He says. May the treasure of God's Word be experienced in your life!

APPLICATION

WORSHIP:

It is hard to remain unthankful when someone gives so much to you out of love. God loves you so much that He has given you His Word to bless you and cause His benefits to shower over your life. Thank Him and praise Him today for so many blessings through His living and powerful Word.

PRAYER:

"Lord, I love your Word. Thank you for blessing me beyond what I can ever imagine. Help me to rely on and trust in your Word. I am blessed by who You are and what You say. I choose to love your Word, live in your Word, and live by your Word. I receive all your blessings and benefits. In Jesus' name. Amen."

DECLARATION:

"I bless the Lord, and through His word do not forget His benefits towards me" (Psalm 103:1-2).

ACTION:

Out of the blessings listed that come from reading and receiving God's Word in your life, which one speaks the most to you now?

What benefit from God's Word do you need today? Choose the top 3 benefits that you desire and need in your life today. Read the promise (associated Scriptures) over and over, until it becomes part of your thinking and makes a home in your heart. Watch how God changes you and changes the circumstances around you!

DAY 3: LIES BIND. TRUTH FREES

Then Jesus said to those Jews who believed Him, "If you abide in My word, you are My disciples indeed. And you shall know the truth, and the truth shall make you free." They answered Him, "We are Abraham's descendants, and have never been in bondage to anyone. How can You say, 'You will be made free'?" Jesus answered them, "Most assuredly, I say to you, whoever commits sin is a slave of sin. And a slave does not abide in the house forever, but a son abides forever. Therefore if the Son makes you free, you shall be free indeed (John 8:31-36).

True freedom will never be accomplished without God's Word. Freedom without truth cannot exist. Truth is found in God's Word, and when one abides in the Word of God, he or she will know (experience) the truth, and freedom follows. How exciting it is to know that no matter what you need freedom from, you can find it in the truth of God's Word!

Within the same chapter of today's passage, Jesus states that the devil, who hates God and anything that God loves, is a liar and the father of lies (John 8:44). There is no truth in the devil. When he speaks a lie, he is speaking his native language. When Satan speaks to you, it is a lie. It may sound good, look good, seem logical, and have the promise of a good life, but it is a lie. He is a deceiver, and when he speaks lies to you, and you fall for it, he puts on his cloak of condemnation. The name *Satan* literally means "accuser" (Revelation 12:10). His filthy plan and purpose for you is to deceive you, watch you fall, and then condemn you. Once he is successful in tempting you and striking where you are weak, he will then find opportunity to continually tempt, lie, and accuse. His voice will contain those condemnations. Satan sends trials to you to wear you down. He will find success over you when you are bound and in prison spiritually, emotionally, mentally, and physically because of the lies you listened to and allowed yourself to heed.

There are voices you may hear from the media, perhaps from your family and friends, from those you work with, and even from those who dislike you which you believe to convey truth, but they are a lie from the devil. Voices that say, "You are not good enough," "You will never make it," "God can't love you now," "No one cares," "You will always be alone," "Freedom will never be experienced," "You're not as good as . . ."

One of the ways you can discern a lie from the truth is twofold. First, if God's Word does not back it up, then it is not the truth. The truth is greater than all of the voices which lie, and is even greater than what you feel. This is part of what is so freeing about God's Word; the truth is not based on what others say or what you feel like for the moment, but it is unchanging. God's Word—or truth—is settled. Since it is unchanging, you can trust in it no matter what others say or how you feel at the moment.

> ## The truth gives you hope, even in the midst of challenging circumstances and the vicious lies.

The second way that you can discern a lie from the truth is that lies leave you without hope. Let's say that the voice of inadequacy speaks to you by saying, "You can't succeed; you've blown it too much. You're not able or worthy." Believing that lie does not cause a person to be motivated to succeed because it pushes down, oppresses, and can be a heavy burden to carry.

The truth, on the other hand, gives you hope, even in the midst of challenging circumstances and the vicious lies. Fear may be taunting a child not to jump in the deep end of the pool, but once the child knows the truth that mom or dad will catch him in the deep end, he is free to jump. The truth set him free to do what *seemed* impossible.

God is calling you to something better. Jesus has provided the way to freedom and has called you to abide in the truth called God's Word. Once you do, you will know the truth and be set free no matter what is trying to lie to you, bind you, or imprison you. Listen to the voice of truth and reject the lies that bind you. You will be free indeed! (John 8:36).

APPLICATION

WORSHIP:

As you worship the Lord, focus on the truth of who He is. The devil may have been painting a wrong picture of God for you. The devil loves to lie about the nature and character of God. As you read the truth about God's love toward you, worship Him and thank Him for wanting to reveal the truth of who He is.

PRAYER:

"Jesus, help me to be a person who reads the Word of God and remains in it. I now see that my freedom is related to soaking up the truth of Your Word like a sponge. Thank You that Your truth crowds out the lies that Satan has been saying to me. I believe what You say and trust Your Word. Thank You for setting me free!"

DECLARATION:

"I know God's truth and it makes me free. I am free indeed!" (John 8:32, 36)

ACTION:

Feelings are created by God, but they were never created as a guide to know what is true or not. Your feelings can be indicators to what you believe. Take notice how you feel during the day today. Do you feel sad, depressed, anxious, or fearful? Why do you feel that way? What is the root cause of your feelings? The reason for why you feel a certain way is related to what you think. And what you think about God, yourself, your situation, etc., is what you will believe. What you believe and think is what will master your life.

Once you are aware of what you are thinking, ask yourself these questions, "What's the truth? What does God's Word say?" This will always lead you to the truth that will set you free.

DAY 4: GREATLY DESIRE
THE WORD

It is the Spirit who gives life; the flesh profits nothing. The words that I speak to you are spirit, and they are life. But there are some of you who do not believe." For Jesus knew from the beginning who they were who did not believe, and who would betray Him. And He said, "Therefore I have said to you that no one can come to Me unless it has been granted to him by My Father." From that time many of His disciples went back and walked with Him no more. Then Jesus said to the twelve, "Do you also want to go away?" But Simon Peter answered Him, "Lord, to whom shall we go? You have the words of eternal life. Also we have come to believe and know that You are the Christ, the Son of the living God" (John 6:63-69).

The higher the value of something or someone to you, the greater the love and desire you will have. For example, if you own an expensive vehicle, you will make sure that it is taken care of. You will make sure that it stays in wonderful condition and will enjoy the way it looks and drives. Why? Because it costs a lot, means a lot to you, and it is valuable. The same goes for a person in your life. If you value someone greatly, you will treat them with respect and love, and make sure that their well-being is first and foremost. You desire to spend time with them, talk with them, listen to them, and enjoy their company. The reason? That person is important and valuable to you.

The same is true with God's Word. The more you see the value it has, the more you will long to spend time reading it. You will hunger and thirst to read and know the Word because you are hungering and thirsting to know Jesus.

Desiring to read and abide in the Word of God comes from the fact that you know it contains truth, but also because you have actually experienced the transformation from knowing the truth of the Word.

Peter was faced with a question from Jesus in John 6. Jesus asked the twelve disciples if they wanted to leave him like the other disciples had decided to walk away from him. Immediately, Peter passionately answered Jesus by saying, "Lord, to whom shall we go? You have the words of eternal life. Also we have come to believe and know that You are the Christ, the Son of the living God" (John 6:68-69). In other words, Peter was saying, "Lord, why in the world would I leave you? You changed my life; I'm a new man! You saved me and set me free. Your words are what have given me life, freedom, and hope. I would never want to go back to from where you saved me from where death and destruction once reigned in my life!" Peter loved the words of Jesus because he not only gained information from His words, but experienced transformation.

Nothing compares to God's Word because they are words that fill you with the life of Christ.

David said in Psalm 119:97, "Oh, how I love your law! It is my meditation all the day." Paul hungered to know Jesus by saying, "Yet indeed I have count all things loss for the excellence of the knowledge of Christ Jesus my Lord...that I may gain Christ....that I may know Him" (Philippians 3:8,10).

Nothing compares to God's Word because they are words that fill you with the life of Christ. Knowing the value of the Word of God and experiencing the power of it in your personal life will cause you to hunger to read it and abide in it more. You will never want to walk away from it. Nothing compares to hearing from God because it has life changing power!

APPLICATION

WORSHIP:

Worship is a powerful indicator that reveals your desire for God. People who are not in the habit of thanking God and worshipping Him consistently are people who don't really hunger and thirst to know Him. God loves you, even if this may be true in your life. Begin today by worshipping Him from your heart and with your lips. God loves authentic worshippers.

PRAYER:

"Jesus, to whom shall I go? You have the words of eternal life! I desire You above all else. Forgive me for the times where I have kept Your Word set aside because I can become distracted and overwhelmed with everyday life. I realize that all I need is in what you promised and have provided for in Your Word. Your Word transforms me and I choose to value Your Word. Thank You for Your tender mercies and love. Knowing You and listening to Your life-changing Word causes me to long for Your Word more and more each day. I want to know You more. I love You, Jesus."

DECLARATION:

"I desire God's Word. He speaks life (John 6:63) and I accept what He says by faith!"

ACTION:

Reflect on the following questions: Do you value the Word of God? How valuable is it? Has God changed you and has He freed you? How have you recently experienced God? Can you honestly say that you hunger to know Jesus more? Are you longing to read God's Word daily? Or is God's Word something that you read casually? Have you walked away from reading the Word of God consistently? If so, have you recognized what has crowded God's

Word out in your life? Ask God to give you a stronger desire for Him and His Word. If needed, confess to Him that your priorities have been wrong and that you will begin to read the Word of God. You will begin to see that as God's Word is priority in your life, it really is not a religious book, but full of powerful and personal application. Understand that when God's Word is not desired, it will not be read. When the reading of God's Word is not valued, you lose. When you hunger and thirst to hear from God, you will be filled (Matthew 5:6).

DAY 5: TAKING TIME

Now Moses was tending the flock of Jethro his father-in-law, the priest of Midian. And he led the flock to the back of the desert, and came to Horeb, the mountain of God. And the Angel of the Lord appeared to him in a flame of fire from the midst of a bush. So he looked, and behold, the bush was burning with fire, but the bush was not consumed. Then Moses said, "I will now turn aside and see this great sight, why the bush does not burn." So when the Lord saw that he turned aside to look, God called to him from the midst of the bush and said, "Moses, Moses!" And he said, "Here I am" (Exodus 3:1-4).

Over the last few days we have taken a look at how God's Word is life-changing. God always changes us for our good and for His glory. Yet we have to wonder what great truths we have missed by not making time to read God's life-changing Word. What blessings have been forfeited? How many times has encouragement that was needed, healing that was desired, or even missed God's leading because we didn't make hearing the voice of God our first desire or practice?

Moses was tending his father-in-law's flock when the Lord appeared to him as a flame of fire in the midst of a bush. The difference between this bush and other bushes was that this bush was completely on fire but wasn't burnt to the ground; it was not consumed. Moses made a decision by saying, "I will now turn aside and see this great sight" (Exodus 3:3). Moses stopped what he was doing to turn aside and see. He made a decision to change what he was accustomed to doing as a shepherd to focus on the bush. What happened when Moses turned aside? God knew He had Moses' attention. When God saw that Moses turned aside to look, He called out to Moses. When Moses chose to stop and turn aside, God saw Moses' attention move toward Himself and then God spoke to Moses. Moses heard the powerful and living words of God, and it changed Moses' destiny! In fact, because of this event, Moses was used to change the destiny of many.

It is crucial to understand that God desires to free you, grow close to you, guide you, bless you, and speak to you daily more than you desire Him. In order to receive all that God wants to give you through His Word, you must choose to stop, turn aside, and read the Word. You must set aside time daily to abide in God's Word if you want Him to speak to you and powerfully transform you. That means you turn off the TV and turn aside to the Word; you shut off the phone and open up the living Word of God; you turn away from what distracts you and turn to the hope and encouragement of God's Word.

In order to receive all that God wants to give you through His Word, you must choose to stop, turn aside, and read the Word.

The devil and the world are loud. Their voices scream, "Go, don't stop, listen to this and that, turn this on, keep going this way, you need to overwork, you need more, did you hear about, you must watch, and so on." When you keep God's Word on the shelf, God's voice will be hard to hear amidst the steady stream of input.

Freedom will never take place apart from hearing the voice of God, and God speaks primarily through what He wrote to you: the Bible. As Moses made time to turn aside and see, God called Moses to great and mighty things and used him to free the children of Israel! God was there ready to speak, but if Moses never turned aside, he would have missed what God wanted to do that day in him and through him.

Are you turning aside to put your focus on God's Word? Are you ready and willing to drown out the loud voices to hear the still, small, yet powerful, voice of God? (1 Kings 19:11-12). Make it your daily desire to turn aside, read, and listen to God's Word.

APPLICATION

WORSHIP:

As you read the Word of God, give thanks to Him for speaking to you. He longs to speak truth and grace into your life to set you free.

PRAYER:

"Lord, enable me not to be so distracted by my schedule and busyness that I don't turn aside to Your Word. I don't want to miss Your voice or Your will. I am thankful that Your voice will be clear so that I will be changed, set free, and empowered to serve You. May I receive all that You desire for my life as I choose to turn aside to the fire of Your Word. In the name of Jesus I pray and believe. Amen."

DECLARATION:

"As I turn aside to hear from God, He speaks to me (Exodus 3:4) and changes my life."

ACTION:

What distracts you from making a choice to sit at the feet of Jesus and listen to what He says in the Word of God? What practical adjustment do you need to do to make this a priority? Do you need to wake up a little earlier? Do you need to make an appointment in your schedule that is non-negotiable? Perhaps spend a half hour in the Word before you go to bed? What can you cut out so you can focus on reading the precious promises of God? Make it happen. Ask your family, friend, or pastor how you can practically keep this as a part of your everyday life. Perhaps they can do it with you to keep you accountable. As you start to read the Bible regularly, you will hear from God and be changed, and then God and His Word is what you will desire more than ever.

PART II: THINK

MEDITATE ON THE WORD OF GOD

DAY 6: THE FIRST PART OF MEDITATION

This Book of the Law shall not depart from your mouth,
but you shall meditate in it day and night, that you may
observe to do according to all that is written in it. For
then you will make your way prosperous, and then you
will have good success (Joshua 1:8).

Meditation is absolutely necessary to receive all that God wants to give you through His Word and to be healed and set free. God commanded Joshua to meditate on the words of God, and there he would find success and would prosper (Joshua 1:8). The Hebrew word for *meditation* in this passage is *hagah*. This word has a two-part meaning to it. The first part of the meaning means "*to have thoughtful deliberation.*" Meditation is not a quick thought about what God is saying to you; it means that you carefully and purposefully think about what truth God is speaking through the passage, what truth God is speaking personally to you, and how this truth is received by faith and applied to your life. God says in Joshua 1:8 to think about the words of God day and night. In other words, thinking on God's Word is to be a lifestyle, not a religious duty.

You must understand that the war over your life starts in your mind. Paul said that though we walk in the flesh or live in physical bodies, our war is not in the physical realm. The devil wars with you in the spiritual realm and he keeps you bound by his deceptive lies which he tries to settle in your thought life. Paul said in 2 Corinthians 10:4 that the weapons of our warfare against the devil are not coming from the physical realm. Scripture reminds us we are mighty in God to destroy strongholds that keep us bound.

One of the first weapons that God instructs us to war against the father of lies with is our mind. The Holy Spirit instructs us in 2 Corinthians 10:5 to take "every thought into captivity to the obedience of Christ." This means that any wrong thought, evil thought, or lie that comes to you for the purpose of defeating you, you must *not let it* reign in your mind. Instead, when you notice thoughts that are in opposition to the truth of God's Word, you take them into captivity. You take every thought that does not come from the voice or heart of God as a prisoner. The lie that looks to keep you in prison, you take to prison. You take authority over that thought and do not allow it to take over your life. It is time to dethrone the lies that have held you captive—this is done by God's truth.

Removing wrong thoughts about God, about yourself, and about others is done by meditating on God's truth. This is why it is so important to read and abide in God's Word. Once you take the time to do that, you meditate on the truth. You think on it, carefully receive it, and apply it to your life. Take the negative and unbiblical lies and make them a prisoner. Lock up the lies that try to lock you up by replacing them with the truth of God's Word, no matter how you feel or what you see naturally. Make every thought subject to Jesus. When the wrong thought comes to you, you reject it because your mind is now Christ's. Whatever thought God wants you to think and that comes from Him is full of freedom! Remove all thoughts that are not in alignment with God's thoughts by meditating on God's Word. Watch what God will do as you meditate upon God's Word.

"But his delight is in the law of the Lord, and in His law he meditates day and night" (Psalm 1:2).

APPLICATION

WORSHIP:

Worship is an expression of love and adoration to God. As you meditate on God's truth, your worship will grow. For example, as you think about Romans 8:38-39, your mind thinks and accepts the truth that nothing can separate you from God's love. As this truth saturates your mind and heart, you will worship and sing praises to God!

PRAYER:

"I ask You, Holy Spirit, to be the protector of my mind. I ask that You will keep me sensitive to Your voice and leading when it comes to anything coming across my mind that is not from God. I know that You lead me into truth and bring to remembrance the Word of God. Thank You, Lord, for loving me enough to show me the truth so I can be free. By Your grace, I can be strong in meditating on Your Word day and night. I receive Your Word by faith and destroy every high and exalted thought that is in competition to You and Your promises. In Jesus' name. Amen!"

DECLARATION:

"All strongholds are destroyed in my life because my mind is captive to Christ who sets me free" (2 Corinthians 10:4-5).

ACTION:

When a wrong thought comes your way, keep it captive; put it in prison. It has no authority over your life. Submit your thoughts to Jesus, so that you think what he thinks. Peace will come over you and a wonderful freedom will be experienced as you meditate on God's Word.

DAY 7: SET YOUR MIND

If then you were raised with Christ, seek those things
which are above, where Christ is, sitting at the right hand
of God. Set your mind on things above, not on things on
the earth (Colossians 3:1-2).

What is your mind set on? In other words, what is the primary focus of your thinking? If you were asked what dominates your thinking, what would you say?

The truth is that whatever your mind is focused on, is who you will become and where you will go. *What* you think is what affects *what* you do, whether negative or positive, lies or truth.

Today's passage encourages us to set, or focus, our minds on things above. We are challenged in this world to put our focus and attention on its lusts rather than to fix our mind on the things of God. As children of God, we have been born again and are new creations in Christ. As new creations that have been set free and forgiven, we must learn to focus on the truth of God's Word. Colossians 3:2 exhorts us to keep our minds on the Lord and His words, not the voices and lies that the world offers.

Freedom is possible when you think the truth of the Word of God; when you set your mind on heavenly things. The apostle Paul goes even further to explain the power of focusing on what is of God. Romans 8:5-6 says that those who set their minds on the flesh, or the natural man, will satisfy fleshly desires by living according to the flesh. On the contrary, if you set your mind on the Spirit of God, you will live according to what the Holy Spirit says. He goes on to say that to be fleshly minded brings death and destruction, but if you are spiritually minded, life and peace follow.

Focus is crucial in becoming free. There is a powerful truth found in Hebrews 12:1-2. Here the scriptures call us to lay down the sin and weights that cause us to be bound in life. Sin can keep you in chains; weights oppress you and keep you bound up. Yet God says to lay them down to experience freedom. "How?" you may ask. Hebrews 12:2 says, "Looking unto Jesus." The word *looking* here is the Greek word *aphorao*. This word means that you have undivided attention toward the one you are focused on. In fact, it means that you are so focused that you look away from all other distractions in order to fix, or set, your gaze on the one object.

Set your mind on Jesus. Look away from all distractions that keep you from setting your mind on things above. Keep God's Word as your focus day and night. Make God your first priority with your mind. As you think on Him, and your mind abides in all the wonderful truths in God's Word, you will shatter the chains that bind you. Earthly and fleshly thinking will be set aside as you experience life, freedom, and peace by keeping your mind on things above.

Your freedom is found at the place of a God-focused mind.

APPLICATION

WORSHIP:

As you worship the Lord for the next few minutes or so, learn to set your mind on who He is. Don't even think of what He has done yet. Just think of His name, His character, His good nature, and sing to Him out of a heart of thanksgiving.

PRAYER:

"Lord, I set my mind on You. Enable me more and more each day to think of You above all else. I desire to know Your truths and meditate on them, always being mindful of You. By Your grace and power, I choose to look away from all that isn't important, and I look to You. I love You and praise Your holy name! Amen."

DECLARATION:

"I have perfect peace because my mind stays on the Lord" (Isaiah 26:3).

ACTION:

Meditation on God's Word is focus. Pick two scriptures that will help you think the truth. Write them out and put them in your pocket today. Take them out and read, abide, and remember them throughout the day. Keep your focus on them. See how your focus on the truth will free you and change your day.

"My son, give attention to my words; Incline your ear to my sayings. Do not let them depart from your eyes; Keep them in the midst of your heart; For they are life to those who find them, And health to all their flesh" (Proverbs 4:20-22).

DAY 8: RENEWING THE MIND

I beseech you therefore, brethren, by the mercies of God, that you present your bodies a living sacrifice, holy, acceptable to God, which is your reasonable service. And do not be conformed to this world, but be transformed by the renewing of your mind, that you may prove what is that good and acceptable and perfect will of God (Romans 12:1-2).

Today's word from God is a powerful principle when it comes to becoming free. You may need freedom from fear, anxiety, insecurity, discouragement, hopelessness, lust, jealousy, unforgiveness, etc. The good news is that transformation comes by renewing your mind. Your mind is renewed when you read and meditate on the Word of God, which is the truth that sets you free. In order to come to the place where you are renewing your mind, you must first recognize that you are in need of freedom and transformation. Once you recognize this, you must present yourself to God by surrendering to Him (v. 1). You will realize that you no longer want to be conformed (fashioned, modeled, patterned) by the world's ideas, philosophies, and lifestyles in opposition to God and His Word. Rather, you begin to substitute submission to the lies of the devil, the world, and your flesh by meditating and abiding in the Word of God.

The word *renew* here is a fantastic word. The Greek word is *anakainosis*, which literally means "restoration" or "renovation." When you think of renovating a room in your house, such as the kitchen, before you are able to put the new in, you must tear down the old part. The areas that are broken, cracked, not useful, or just not looking good anymore experience the tear-down. They get demolished. The same is true with your thought life. The first step to renewing your mind is smashing and throwing out the old thinking, the thoughts that are broken and break you. You have to recognize the lies that have been sitting in your mind for years and have been keeping you bound. You may ask, "How do I know what thoughts are not from God?" Open up the Word of God and compare what God says to what the wrong thought is saying and repeating in your mind. Part of renovation includes emptying out the old.

The next step is where many have attempted to be free, but to no avail. The reason is that they may be recognizing the old thoughts that are keeping them from being free and they throw them out, but they never finish the renovation. In order to complete the renovation, the new must be built. Building into your mind the new way of thinking through replacing the old thoughts with the words of God is absolutely necessary each day. When you knock down the old thought, replace it with the truth of God's Word. Renovating is not a one-day event. Paul instructs us in Romans 12:2 to renew our mind. This is an ongoing, daily action. This is why meditation is part of renewing. We are to meditate on God's Word all the time (Joshua 1:8). Renewing the mind is continual renovation. It is a lifelong project to remove the lies and replace them with God's truths.

> ### Your words, actions, and lifestyle are transformed by the renewing—or renovation—of your thinking.

What's the promise of renovation and restoration of our minds? Transformation! This word in the Greek is *metamorphoo*. This word means "to transfigure or change one's outward appearance." This is the same Greek word used in Matthew 17:2 and Mark 9:2 when Jesus' appearance transfigured, or transformed, before Peter, James, and John!

What a powerful principle of meditating on the Word of God! The evidence of being set free is by a changed outward manifestation. Your words, actions, and lifestyle are transformed by the renewing—or renovation—of your thinking. And renewed thinking comes by meditating on the life-changing Word of God!

I was never the life of the party, nor have I ever had a type-A personality. I tend to be loving and personal with people, and I enjoy getting to know new people, but my personality tends to be more laid back in nature. This posed a problem when God called me to be a minister and preach the Word of God. When I started to sense the call to full-time ministry as a teenager, I did not say yes right away because I felt completely inadequate and insufficient to do such a thing. I hated speaking in front of people. In fact, whenever I knew I had to read a paragraph or two in front of the class in school, I dreaded it. I would sweat, shake, and my voice would tremble when talking because I was gripped with fear. When I finally came to surrender to the will of God, I had to renew my thinking when it came to public speaking. The Holy Spirit led me to 1 Corinthians 2:1-5. I began to meditate on this passage and rely on this truth when it came time to preach and teach. Doing so allowed me to focus on God's ability to work through me, despite my weakness and inability on my own. As my mind was renewed and renovated with this truth, I began to follow God with boldness and great desire. Today, this scripture is a guiding light as I obey the call of God on my life.

Choose to renew your mind today. Remove the old and ugly lies, and replace them with the new; the truth. You will find a new way of living fully free.

APPLICATION

WORSHIP:

Thank God for being a good God. He has come to restore your life by restoring your mind. Worship Him for being a wonderful healer and restorer.

PRAYER:

"Jesus, thank You for your Word. I praise Your name for giving me Your Word, which is truth. I receive what You say and I throw out old thoughts that have kept me down and defeated in life. Your Word frees me from the inside so I can be changed on the outside. Help me to live out Your Word more as I meditate on what You say about me. I worship You with my mind and know that You are transforming me. Restore me and renovate my mind for Your glory! In the name of Jesus. Amen."

DECLARATION:

"I will not conform to the world or what it says to me, but am transformed by the renewing of my mind" (Romans 12:2).

ACTION:

Renewing the mind is renovating the mind. Renovating includes demolition and rebuilding. The Holy Spirit wants you to be free, so He will help you by revealing the wrong thoughts and giving you the redeemed thoughts from His Word. On a piece of paper, make a list of five to ten thoughts that keep you bound and are not what God says. Across from the false thought, write out God's Word that combats the lie. This way you will begin to renew, or renovate, your mind. Meditate and focus on the truth that destroys the lie.

Examples:

- False thought: "God does not love me anymore."
  Truth: "The cross shows God's unfailing love for me"
  (1 John 4:19).

- False thought: "God doesn't want me to prosper."
  Truth: "God's plan and purpose for my life is to prosper"
  (Jeremiah 29:11).

- False thought: "It's too hard."
  Truth: "There is nothing too hard for God" (Jeremiah 32:17).

- False thought: "I will always be defeated."
  Truth: "Jesus has made me a conquerer; I have victory through Him now (Romans 8:37).

DAY 9: YOU ARE WHAT YOU THINK

For as he thinks in his heart, so *is* he. "Eat and drink!" he says to you, but his heart is not with you (Proverbs 23:7).

But you have not so learned Christ, if indeed you have heard Him and have been taught by Him, as the truth is in Jesus: that you put off, concerning your former conduct, the old man which grows corrupt according to the deceitful lusts, and be renewed in the spirit of your mind, and that you put on the new man which was created according to God, in true righteousness and holiness (Ephesians 4:20-24).

Thoughts are powerful. Thoughts affect who you become, whether negative thoughts or positive thoughts. If you entertain false thinking, negative thoughts, and have a habit of thinking what is untrue, you will begin to act out and become that way. On the contrary, if you obey the command to meditate on God's truth continually, it is a positive influence that will permeate your heart, your words, and how you live.

For example, if you are someone who struggles with fear, you are bombarded with thoughts that keep you trapped. These thoughts of insecurity attack you to keep you from experiencing God's best, stop you from taking steps of faith, and can even keep you from amazing relationships that will cause you to be encouraged in your faith. You have become afraid because you are listening to the wrong voices that sow lies in your mind. Thoughts such as, "You will never make it. No one cares what you are doing. This will never become a success. If you take that step, what will others think of you? You don't deserve to be blessed." Once you accept these seeds of fear, you reap the consequences. You become exactly what you think, and you are unable to experience the freedom that comes from knowing the truth about God and yourself.

On the other hand, it is so powerful to read, meditate, and accept what God thinks of you. Freedom comes to you when you allow the seed of the Word of God to be planted in your mind. God's thoughts toward you are good! Psalm 139:17 -18 says, "How precious also are Your thoughts to me, O God! How great is the sum of them! If I should count them, they would be more in number than the sand." Wow! God's good thoughts about you and toward you are more than all the grains of sand in the world! Jeremiah 29:11 says that God's thoughts toward you are "peace and not of evil, to give you a future *and a hope!*" Receiving even those two passages and making them a part of your daily thought life will begin to transform your mind and heart. Once they do, it removes the old, fearful way of thinking because you know and ponder continually God's truth of God's great purpose and plan for your life.

Your words and actions are indicators of what you have allowed to make a home in your mind.

The result of thinking and meditating on what God thinks and says, is that you live it out. You live out God's ways because you think the way God thinks. Meditating on God's thoughts gives you freedom in the life God intended you to live. No longer will you live trapped and imprisoned by negative lies, but you excel and run forward in the freedom of truth.

Do you believe the truth of who God says you are as His child, or do you have a low self-esteem coupled with guilt and shame? Is there a struggle in your life that you just can't seem to overcome? Are you on an emotional roller coaster; one moment you are up, the next down? Does it seem to you that you are over-critical, complaining, and negative with what you say throughout the day? Are you filled with doubt about what you know you should do?

Check your thinking; you are what you think. Your words and actions are indicators of what you have allowed to make a home in your mind. Cut off the lies that are keeping you trapped, and allow the seed of God's Word be planted, grow, and flourish in your mind. You will find yourself becoming free in the "good and acceptable and perfect will of God" (Romans 12:2).

APPLICATION

WORSHIP:

Sing to the Lord, who never changes. He is faithful, good, and loving forever. As you worship God and are in His presence, allow Him to reveal His precious thoughts toward you.

PRAYER:

"Jesus, I want to know You and know Your thoughts toward me. Reveal the wrong thoughts that I have been thinking for so long. I confess them to You and today I choose to listen to what You say and Your promises over my life. As I think on You and receive Your words/thoughts, I will become like You. Thank You for setting me free!"

DECLARATION:

"I am an imitator of God because I am His child and am renewing the spirit of my mind" (Ephesians 5:1; 4:23).

ACTION:

Who you want to become is your choice. You become what you meditate on, whether lies that bind or truth that makes you free. You go where your mind goes. Make a choice to meditate on God's Word and receive His thoughts toward you today. Draw a line in the sand and choose His voice and make those words your thoughts. Read Joshua 24:15-16, 24.

DAY 10: THINK ON THESE THINGS

Finally, brethren, whatever things are true, whatever things are noble, whatever things are just, whatever things are pure, whatever things are lovely, whatever things are of good report, if there is any virtue and if there is anything praiseworthy—meditate on these things. The things which you learned and received and heard and saw in me, these do, and the God of peace will be with you (Philippians 4:8-9).

We have seen how important it is to think on, meditate upon, and ponder God's Word. Today's scripture gives us even further instruction on what to focus on as we live each day. God's Word itself is what we need to meditate on, but He also gives us guidelines for our thinking. There are specific characteristics of what God says must be the focus of our minds. It is clear and concise—and when adhered to, will cause us to have great peace and freedom. When our minds stray from thinking about these characteristics and we allow ourselves to think what is contrary to them, we will be deceived and caught in a trap without even knowing we have been caught.

Often, compromising on these principles of the mind trap us through what we see, watch, or read. This should not be a surprise because Jesus said, "The lamp of the body is the eye. If therefore your eye is good, your whole body will be full of light. But if your eye is bad, your whole body will be full of darkness" (Matthew 6:22-23). Once we choose to see, watch, and read what is contrary to this passage, our minds will begin to think, meditate, and ponder that which will ultimately control us and keep us in bondage.

What does God call us to meditate on? The focus He commands can be found in Philippians 4:8 (NESV):

- "Whatever is true." *True* means "that which is correct, worthy of credit, honest."

- "Whatever is honorable." *Honorable* means" that which is reputable, dignified."

- "Whatever is just." *Just* means "that which is upright, righteous, innocent."

- "Whatever is pure." *Pure* means "that which is modest, chaste, blameless."

- "Whatever is lovely." *Lovely* means "that which is acceptable."

- "Whatever is commendable." This means "that which is a good report, reputable."

- "If there is any excellence." This means "a good quality, goodness, virtue."

- "If there is anything worthy of praise." *Praise* means "applause, honor due, commendation."

God calls us to meditate on these things. He wants us to make it a priority to ponder and think on these. The question is, what can you think of that does not make the list of these amazing qualities? What do you allow your eyes to see, read, and watch that cause your mind to focus on what is harmful to your heart and life? The truth is, God has given us these wonderful qualities and characteristics to meditate on for our own good. The lie is that when we keep to these, we will not enjoy life. On the contrary, God declares that we will enjoy true peace as we meditate on these things.

You can always count on God's Word to be true, honorable, just, pure, lovely, commendable, excellent, and worthy of praise. This is what must be counted on for meditation, including a guideline as we live day to day in this world. You will never be disappointed in keeping God's words and His voice priority. It will set you free!

> You will never be disappointed in keeping God's words and His voice priority. It will set you free!

APPLICATION

WORSHIP:

As you worship God, thank Him for His love for you. He loves you enough to guide you into what is right and good to meditate on. In fact, God himself has these characteristics. Worship Him for who He is to you!

PRAYER:

"Oh, Lord, how I desire to think, focus, and meditate upon Your directives. Forgive me for allowing my eyes and ears to accept what is far from what You have created and designed for me to see and hear. As I look to You and Your Word, help me to stay focused on words of life. May anything that is in conflict with what You speak of in Philippians 4:8 become empty to me. Your Word is a guard and protector of my eyes and ears, of my mind and heart. As I meditate on these things, I rejoice at You and thank You for freeing me!"

DECLARATION:

"I meditate on what is true, noble, just, pure, lovely, of good report, virtuous, and praiseworthy" (Philippians 4:8).

ACTION:

What can you get rid of or stop seeing and hearing that discourages you from meditating on what God listed? Entertainment? Books? Music? Ungodly conversation with anyone you hang out with? An app? Website? Don't be deceived. Freedom, joy, and happiness are found in being full of the Holy Spirit as you meditate on what is right. Remember, you become what you think. What is filling your mind? What dominates your thought life? Ask the Holy Spirit to reveal things that do not belong and fill your focus with God's Word.

PART III: SPEAK

Declare the Word of God

DAY 11: THE 2ND PART OF MEDITATION

This Book of the Law shall not depart from your mouth,
but you shall meditate in it day and night, that you may
observe to do according to all that is written in it. For
then you will make your way prosperous, and then you
will have good success (Joshua 1:8).

But his delight is in the law of the Lord, and in His law
he meditates day and night. (Psalm 1:2).

When God commanded Joshua to enter the Promised Land He gave encouraging words to Joshua. He told him to be strong and courageous and not to be discouraged nor to fear, for God was with Him. God also instructed Joshua to do something with the words of the Law, which we touched on in Part II. As you recall, God tells Joshua, "This Book of the Law shall not depart from your mouth, but you shall meditate in it day and night, that you may observe to do according to all that is written in it. For then you will make your way prosperous, and then you will have good success" (Joshua 1:8).

We have talked about how it is God's will for us to meditate on the Word of God over the last five days. We looked at how the word *meditation* means that we should think and ponder on the truth of the Word of God for our own life. That is the first part of the definition of *meditation* and is crucial for our freedom.

The second part of what it means to meditate is found in today's scripture. Notice what God says to Joshua about His Word. God's words "shall not depart from your **mouth**." The Hebrew word, *peh*, means exactly what it says, *your mouth, command, or your speech*. Joshua 1:8 says not to let the Word of God stop coming out of your mouth, but rather you need to continue to…meditate. You may think the verse should have said, "Do not let the word of God depart from your mouth, but keep speaking it." Well, you're right! God said not to allow His words to depart from your mouth, or from speaking it, but you shall meditate on it day and night. Remember, the word *meditate* here is *hagah*, which means "to think and ponder." What's important to understand is this Hebrew word also means "to mutter, to speak to oneself that comes from thoughtful deliberation." God is saying to Joshua, "Do not let my words depart from your mouth. Meditate on my words day and night. Think of my words, ponder over my words, speak my words, give voice to my words, declare my words to yourself, so that you can obey it and be successful." So we see that meditation and speaking are synonymous.

> ## The individual who delights in the Word of God by thinking about and speaking the Word of God is promised to be blessed!

There is such wonderful freedom when you practice meditating on God's Word, particularly by speaking the Word of God. God's Word is not meant to be kept quiet or bottled up. That is why God fashioned the meaning of *meditation* to convey not only thinking and focusing on the truth that sets us free, but also declaring it over the lives and circumstances of ourselves and others.

The individual who delights in the Word of God by thinking about and speaking the Word of God is promised to be blessed! Don't let God's words fail to come from your lips. When you keep the Word of God continually before you, you will think and speak it all day and night. Watch what awesome things God will reveal, say, and do in and through your life as you start speaking, or meditating, upon the Word of God.

APPLICATION

WORSHIP:

Give God glory and honor. As you sing to Him and worship Him, thank Him for revealing the power of His words through biblical meditation. Declare His goodness out loud!

PRAYER:

"Jesus, I love You. Thank You for the awesome privilege of knowing Your Word! I am so thrilled to know that I not only receive Your truth in my heart, but I can declare it over and over in meditation. Lead me in Your Word that helps me to overcome _____. I will choose to read and think and speak it over my life. As I declare Your powerful truth, I am free!"

DECLARATION:

"I do not allow the words of God to depart from my mouth. I think the Word and speak it" (Joshua 1:8).

ACTION:

Pick out three verses that minister to you, encourage you, and help you become free in Christ. Write them out on an index card or piece of paper. Carry it with you throughout the day. Read it, focus on it, and speak it out loud over and over. Let it become a part of your routine and way of life.

DAY 12: THE CREATIVE POWER OF GOD'S WORD

In the beginning God created the heavens and the earth. The earth was without form, and void; and darkness was on the face of the deep. And the Spirit of God was hovering over the face of the waters. Then God said, "Let there be light"; and there was light (Genesis 1:1-3).

For the promise that he would be the heir of the world was not to Abraham or to his seed through the law, but through the righteousness of faith. Therefore it is of faith that it might be according to grace, so that the promise might be sure to all the seed, not only to those who are of the law, but also to those who are of the faith of Abraham, who is the father of us all (as it is written, "I have made you a father of many nations") in the presence of Him whom he believed—God, who gives life to the dead and calls those things which do not exist as though they did; who, contrary to hope, in hope believed, so that he became the father of many nations, according to what was spoken, "So shall your descendants be" (Romans 4:13, 16-18).

God never speaks anything that is untrue, in vain, or that has no purpose. God's Word is not empty, but full of life and power. When speaking about God's words, the prophet Isaiah says, "For as the rain comes down, and the snow from heaven, and do not return there, but water the earth, and make it bring forth and bud, that it may give seed to the sower and bread to the eater, so shall my word be that goes forth from My mouth; it shall not return to Me void, but it shall accomplish what I please, and it shall prosper in the thing for which I sent it" (Isaiah 55:10-11). God's words are sown when they are spoken, and when we speak what comes out of God's mouth, God works powerfully to accomplish His amazing and loving purposes.

The power of God's words, or what God says, is clearly seen in the creation of this world. When the earth had no form and it was void and dark, God changed its condition by speaking. Genesis 1:3 says, "God said." The word in the original language for *said* means exactly what it means. The word *said* in this verse means "to say, command, utter, speak." When God commanded that there be light, He audibly spoke those words. When God spoke those words out of His mouth, what used to be void, empty, dark, and formless began to dramatically change. God spoke and His words created and formed things because the words that come from God's mouth come from God's unchanging nature.

Abraham was called to get out of his country, away from his family, to a land of blessing. God said that Abraham would be the father of many nations (Genesis 12:1-3; 17:1-6). The problem was that in the natural, Abraham and Sarah were beyond the years of childbearing. Their problem in the natural was like the description of earth in Genesis 1:2; it was dark, void, and there was no form. The natural circumstance said to Abraham and Sarah that it was impossible because of what was seen, heard, and experienced in the natural. Their natural circumstance was called barrenness, childless, they were too old. Though this natural reality was the circumstance, God still called him *Abraham*, which means "father of many." God changed Abram's name to Abraham (Genesis 17:5) and continually called him that because that is what God promised with His mouth.

Speaking of Abraham, the apostle Paul said, "God, who gives life to the dead and calls those things which do not exist as though they did; who contrary to hope, in hope believed, so that he became the father of many nations, according to what was spoken" (Romans 4:17-18). Did you get that? Even when Abraham did not have any children from Sarah at all, God spoke creative words of power by calling him the father of many nations. God changed Abram's name and changed the destiny of Abraham because God promised it. And Abraham put His faith in what God said and today the fruit of God's promise to Abraham is still being realized through those who have put their faith in Jesus Christ (Galatians 3:29). The blessing to and through Abraham came because God spoke his word of promise and called Abraham by the name of promise, even when the natural circumstances spoke otherwise.

> God spoke His words so that you can speak His words. They have creative power to destroy that which is keeping you bound in order to set you free in His will and great purposes.

What is void, dark, and lifeless in your life? God has spoken out of his mouth many precious promises for you (2 Peter 1:4). What is important to understand is that God's spoken word is powerful and sets the prisoner free. It raises the dead, heals the sick, destroys the chains that bind, and brings purpose to your life where there once was emptiness. His spoken word will change your name and your destiny as it did for Abraham.

Your freedom in Christ is found when you speak God's Word. God spoke His words so that you can speak His words. They have creative power to destroy that which is keeping you bound in order to set you free in His will and great purposes. Do not keep silent. Audibly speak, say, and utter God's words over your life and to your circumstance. "Let the redeemed of the Lord say so" (Psalm 107:2).

APPLICATION

WORSHIP:

Worship God out loud. Sing to Him. Declare his lovingkindness and goodness to you. Worship Him for His powerful words!

PRAYER:

Pray out loud: "Jesus, I love You! Help me to understand and obey the power of speaking Your Word out loud. I see that Your Word was never meant to keep quiet, but to be declared and spoken. Thank You for speaking to me through Your Word. I will declare to myself (meditate) and to others Your powerful words! Thank You for Your freedom and life that You have promised me. In Jesus' name. Amen."

DECLARATION:

"I declare from my mouth what God said out of His mouth" (Psalm 119:13).

ACTION:

Practice speaking the Word of God out loud. Read the scripture for today's devotional out loud. The more you meditate (think and speak) on God's Word, the more it becomes part of your thinking and speaking. You will find yourself speaking God's Word in your time of need because it has become a lifestyle and habit. All the power of darkness is disarmed and put to flight when God's powerful words are declared. It is light that expels the darkness.

DAY 13: JESUS, OUR EXAMPLE

Now when the tempter came to Him, he said, "If You are the Son of God, command that these stones become bread." But He answered and said, "It is written, 'Man shall not live by bread alone, but by every word that proceeds from the mouth of God' " (Matthew 4:3-4).

One of the greatest characteristics of God is that He will never tell you to do something that He does not do already. God is not a hypocrite. He lives the way He calls you to live.

This also applies to declaring the Word of God. In today's scripture, Jesus shows how brilliant He is! He teaches us how to overcome the devil and live in freedom by showing us and revealing to us that we must speak God's Word out loud. When temptation comes, nothing is more important than speaking the Word of God out of our mouths.

In Matthew 4:1-11, we find the story of how Jesus was tempted by the devil. Jesus had just finished fasting forty days and forty nights. The devil, who is called the tempter in this passage, tempted Jesus to use His power and authority for His own needs. The devil commanded Jesus to turn the stones into bread. Jesus did not resist the devil by thinking about how to overcome him or by quietly thinking about God's Word. Matthew 4:4 says, "But He answered and **said**, "It is written, 'Man shall not live by bread alone, but by every word that proceeds from the mouth of God.'"

First of all, Jesus *said*. This means that Jesus actually spoke out the answer. The answer to the devil was not just hidden in His heart. Jesus was vocal. Secondly, Jesus went to the Word of God. He said, "It is written." Jesus did not argue with the devil, try to convince the devil what He thought, or even scream at the devil to get away. Jesus went straight to the Word of God. In fact, He went directly to God's Word the other two times that the devil tempted Him during this testing period.

The first scripture that Jesus used was from Deuteronomy 8:3. It says that man lives not just by eating natural bread, but by speaking God's Word, which gives true life. The word used here for *word* is the Greek word *rhema*. This is a powerful word in the Greek. This word means "that which is spoken, a declaration, an utterance." A rhema word is God's word that is given to you by the Holy Spirit in your time of need. It is a portion of God's Word that you declare out loud in time of temptation, when the lies of the enemy come to you, when you need to overcome, and when you are putting your faith in what God says for your freedom. When the time comes, you speak out that rhema word against the enemy who tries to keep you from freedom and God's purpose.

> Jesus was not only teaching us to declare the Word of God and to give voice to God's words, but He was also being an example.

The amazing truth about this passage is that Jesus uses this scripture to teach us to declare God's Word against the devil's schemes, lies, and temptation against us. What makes this even more amazing is that while Jesus was teaching us this verse, He was practicing this principle at the same time! Jesus was not only teaching us to declare the Word of God and to give voice to God's words, but He was also being an example. He was practicing what He was preaching! As He declared what is written in the Word of God to the devil, He used the scripture to teach us that we must also speak the Word for the life of freedom that God intends for us to live.

As Jesus spoke God's words and was victorious over the devil, so we will be victorious as we live by every rhema, spoken word "that proceeds from the mouth of God."

APPLICATION

WORSHIP:

Honor and adore Jesus for the revelation of God's spoken words. Worship Jesus for His perfect example of winning the battle through the written and spoken Word. Sing loud and unashamed before Him.

PRAYER:

"Jesus, I want to follow You. As I do, I will defeat the enemy in my life by knowing Your Word and declaring it in my time of need and temptation. Thank You that the power of Your Word is what needs to be spoken out loud to defeat the devil's lies. I will say out loud, "It is written." Holy Spirit, as I live my life by meditating (thinking and speaking) the Word, I trust You to give me the rhema words to set me free in my time of need.

DECLARATION:

"I do not live by bread alone, but by every spoken word of God that comes from His mouth and is released out of my mouth" (Matthew 4:4).

ACTION:

Notice your struggles and the temptation that comes to you. Wherever you are weak, look up scriptures that are associated with that weakness. Abide in God's Word concerning this, and speak it out loud when you are faced with temptation. When the devil comes to compromise your freedom, immediately declare God's life-changing Word.

DAY 14: SPEAK TO THE MOUNTAIN

Now in the morning, as He returned to the city, He was hungry. And seeing a fig tree by the road, He came to it and found nothing on it but leaves, and said to it, "Let no fruit grow on you ever again." Immediately the fig tree withered away. And when the disciples saw it, they marveled, saying, "How did the fig tree wither away so soon?" So Jesus answered and said to them, "Assuredly, I say to you, if you have faith and do not doubt, you will not only do what was done to the fig tree, but also if you say to this mountain, 'Be removed and be cast into the sea,' it will be done. And whatever things you ask in prayer, believing, you will receive" (Matthew 21:18-22).

God's precious Word continually shows us the power of speaking what God tells us to speak. He shows us to speak His words over the things that are a struggle, dead, or in opposition to the will of God. Because transformation comes when God speaks, He calls us to speak His words so transformation and freedom can be manifested in our lives and in other people's lives.

The prophet Ezekiel was led by the Spirit of the Lord and was set down in the midst of a valley full of dry bones. The Lord commanded Ezekiel to do something that is so powerful. He told Ezekiel, "Prophesy to these bones, and **say** to them, 'O dry bones, hear the word of the Lord! Thus says the Lord God'" (Ezekiel 37:4-5). In this instance, God did not tell Ezekiel to pray all night, but instead to speak to the dry bones. God himself didn't speak to the bones, but He gave Ezekiel full authority to speak to the dry bones. When Ezekiel obeyed God and spoke, God did the miracle!

Jesus, being hungry, passed by a fig tree. Finding no fruit on it, Jesus spoke out loud to the fig tree and said it would not to grow fruit ever again. He *spoke* to a fig tree. He spoke to that which was in opposition to what He needed. Mark 11:14 also gives this account, and says, "And His disciples heard it." They heard Jesus speak to the fig tree. Matthew says that the fig tree immediately withered away and the disciples saw it. They marveled and asked the big question we ask when we are not in full faith; they asked, "how did this happen?" Jesus goes on to say that if you have faith and *say* to the mountain that is in front of you to be removed, it will be removed as you speak in faith. Jesus is teaching us that we are to speak to the mountains, which are the impossibilities in the natural, by hearing God's Word and declaring what He says over it. When you *speak*, you will *see*.

God is calling you to speak the Word of God—the truth—over your dry bones and the mountains that stand in your way.

One day Peter and John were headed to the temple for prayer around three o'clock in the afternoon. A man who had been lame from birth lay at the gate of the temple, asking for alms as people walked by. He did the same as Peter and John walked by. Peter looked at the lame man, asked that the lame man to look at him, and he said to the lame man, "Silver and gold I do not have, but what I do have I give to you: In the name of Jesus Christ of Nazareth, rise up and walk" (Acts 3:6). The lame man was healed and began walking, leaping, and praising God. Peter didn't fast and pray all week wondering what he should do for the lame man. Peter walked with Jesus for about three years; he remembered what Jesus did. He remembered the fig tree and Jesus' instruction to speak to the mountain. Peter remembered that Jesus has all authority in heaven and on earth and commissioned all disciples with this authority. On the basis of remembering and receiving from Jesus, Peter spoke to the mountain. He commanded the mountain of physical infirmity to be healed in the name of Jesus. Peter spoke out loud to the mountain, and God did the miraculous!

I will never forget how God showed me how powerful the principle of speaking His Word out loud is. It was my first year in Bible college and I was part of a prison ministry with two other classmates. Each Monday night we would head to a medium security prison, hand out stapled pages of hymns/choruses to sing out worship songs, and then we would rotate each week to preach the Word of God. The Holy Spirit moved powerfully as many men came to know Jesus and began to grow in the Word of God.

On one particular Monday night, it was my turn to preach. As I was preaching, a tall, intimidating, and particularly muscular gentleman stood up right in the middle of my preaching, yelled at the man sitting across from him, spewed curse words at him, and told him to shut up because he was "trying to hear the preacher!" Well, the man getting yelled at did not put up with that, so he stood up and got in the other man's face. They began to scream at one another and were ready to fight. In fact, it led the whole cafeteria to stand to their feet to get ready to fight. All fifty-five of them completely forgot that I was there to preach, and a brawl was about to go down! What did I do? I comically said, "Guys, can you please sit down?" I, along with my two partners in ministry from college stood still, not knowing what to do or what to expect next.

Suddenly, the Holy Spirit spoke quickly and powerfully to me. As things intensified and the guards were beginning to open the prison doors to come in, God told me to speak out loud from 1 John 4:19, "We love Him because He first loved us." I repeatedly kept speaking this rhema word out loud. The more I spoke it, the more I spoke from the authority of God. As I kept speaking it, suddenly the whole room got quiet—it was as if they were in a trance. They forgot what they were about to do and began to all look at me in unison, and they quietly sat down to listen to the rest of the message. Many of the men came up when I called them to respond, and we prayed over them. The word of God was spoken over my time of need and a circumstance that needed help from God. I spoke the word of God to the mountain, and the mountain was thrown into the sea.

God is calling you to speak the Word of God—the truth—over your dry bones and the mountains that stand in your way. Speak His Word out loud in faith and watch the hand of the Lord do the miraculous in your life. Freedom is found in speaking the inspired and inerrant Word of God!

APPLICATION

WORSHIP:

Find a worship song that you love singing to the Lord. Let this song and melody stay in your heart all day. Worship God for being a powerful God!

PRAYER:

"Lord, I come to You today and I see the powerful truth of speaking Your words in faith and with authority. Thank You for being my shelter. I put my trust in You that as I speak Your powerful words over my dry bones and mountains, no matter how overwhelming they may seem, I am confident that hope will transform that lifeless situation and the mountains will fall in your presence. I believe the same word which You spoke to create the universe is the word that You give me to shatter the kingdom of darkness's power over my life and in the lives of others. Thank You, Jesus, for my freedom! I believe You are Lord and thank You, in Your name. Amen."

DECLARATION:

"I say to this mountain, 'Be removed and be cast into the sea.' I do not doubt in my heart but believe what I say to it. I have whatever I say to the mountain because God tells me to say it." (Mark 11:23)

ACTION:

First, you must know and acknowledge the dry bones and mountains in your life. Is it a disease, financial problem, a sin habit, emotional pain, false accusations toward you, or even wrong thought patterns? Now speak God's words that wars against these lies and natural struggles. Speak to your dry bones, declare with authority the Word of God to the mountain. God is faithful to His Word; be faithful in speaking the Word for your freedom. Remember, speaking God's Word to your mountain may seem awkward at first, but Jesus spoke to the fig tree, and He tells you to speak to your mountain.

DAY 15: THE SWORD OF THE SPIRIT

Above all, taking the shield of faith with which you will
be able to quench all the fiery darts of the wicked one.
And take the helmet of salvation, and the sword of the
Spirit, which is the word of God (Ephesians 6:16-17).

The Holy Spirit inspired the apostle Paul in Ephesians 6:10-18 to teach that we are certainly in a war. But the war for our freedom is not with people; our war is with the demonic spirits, wicked spirits that hate God and hate you. With that being known, God does not leave us to fight on our own. He has given us armor for combat to win the battles in our lives. The crucial weapon of the spiritual warfare that we are looking at today is the sword of the Spirit, which Paul says is the Word of God (Ephesians 6:17).

The sword was a common and main weapon for fighting battles during Paul's time. The believers in the church of Ephesus, who Paul was writing to in this letter, knew exactly of the lethal power of a sword. They specifically knew what kind of sword Paul was referring to here. It conjured images of terror and certain defeat. The Greek word for *sword* here is *machaira*. This was the most vicious sword used in the Roman empire. This sword was the sword of execution. It was a shorter sword that was like a dagger. The *machaira* sword was a two-edged sword and was curved at the end or would have an end that was like the end of the cork screw. When this sword was plunged into the opponent's body, it would penetrate because it was razor sharp, and would be twisted in the body so that it would pull out the insides of the enemy's organs. This is why it was a fierce and feared weapon. This is the sword that Paul was describing as the weapon that defeats Satan.

Paul goes on to say that this sword which is lethal to the enemy and will execute the spiritual forces of wickedness is the *Word of God*. The Greek word used here for *word* is the same word we saw Jesus use in Matthew 4:4. Jesus used the sword of the Spirit against the devil, the *rhema*, or *spoken* word of God! Paul is saying here that in order to do battle against the devil and the hosts of wickedness, you must use the sword of execution and death; the spoken word of God. When you speak God's Word, you defeat the devil, the lies he speaks, and the wrong thoughts that he shares with you. The enemy fears this sword because it exposes, rebukes, renounces, and rejects the lies that keep you captive. The sword of the Spirit—the declared words of God—is the weapon that causes the sick to be healed, the bound to be set free, the lost to come to know Jesus, and the heart to be at peace.

> The sword of the Spirit—the declared words of God—are the weapon that causes the sick to be healed, the bound to be set free, the lost to come to know Jesus, and the heart to be at peace.

The problem is you may not be free because you have kept your sword in your sheath during the battle. The enemy has harassed you, lied to you, and attacked you so that you stay stuck and bound. God has given you His Word to speak, but you remain quiet because you may not have been taking the sword out to even read it. Purpose in your heart today to read, abide, meditate, and declare God's Word. Take it out of your sheath and attack the enemy. You will experience freedom daily as you use the sword of the Spirit, declaring the truth of God's Word that will always set you free.

APPLICATION

WORSHIP:

As you worship the Lord, sing the words of God by finding a portion of the Psalms. Make a melody to the Lord. Thank Him and love on the Lord for giving you His Word.

PRAYER:

"I thank You, Lord, for giving me the sword of the Spirit, which is Your spoken Word. Empower me to always be mindful of Your Word and declare it in my time of testing. I know that I am in a war, but I praise You for giving me the weapon that will bring fear to the enemy and defeat him. I receive Your Word and Your power as I take out the Word from my sheath and crush the lies of the devil, the world, and my flesh. In Jesus' name. Amen."

DECLARATION:

"I take my sword and attack with the truth of the Word of God by declaring it out of my mouth."

ACTION:

Don't keep silent. Speaking the Word out loud against the lies that bind you is a great weapon that fights for freedom. No matter what the circumstances, feelings you may have, or what you see in the natural, speak to the wind and waves with God's Word.

PART IV: APPLY

Receive the blood of Jesus

DAY 16: FREED THROUGH THE BLOOD

For I will pass through the land of Egypt on that night, and will strike all the firstborn in the land of Egypt, both man and beast; and against all the gods of Egypt I will execute judgment: I am the Lord. Now the blood shall be a sign for you on the houses where you are. And when I see the blood, I will pass over you; and the plague shall not be on you to destroy you when I strike the land of Egypt (Exodus 12:12-14).

The children of Israel were suffering under Egyptian bondage (Exodus 2:23). They were not free, so they cried out to the Lord out of the suffering from the bondage that they were in. Being such a good God, He heard their cries (Exodus 2:24-25). God hated that they were in bondage and not free. God hates that you struggle and suffer with bondage; He has heard your cries. The Lord loves you and has committed His life to you so you can live and stay free. As He freed the children of Israel, He has freed you.

In Exodus 12:1-14, God gave Moses instructions and good news on how He would free the children of Israel from slavery and the bitterness of hard bondage. He commanded each family in Israel to take a lamb without blemish and to kill it at a certain time, so that the whole congregation would be killing a lamb at the same time. After the lambs were slaughtered, the children of Israel were to take some of the blood and to apply it on the two doorposts and on the lintel of the houses. God's judgment would come upon unrepentant Pharaoh and the land of Egypt by killing all their firstborn. Judgment would not come upon any house where God saw the blood on the doorposts and the lintel. In essence, He would pass over any household that had applied the blood of the lamb. Thus, the Passover was instituted, for God saved Israel from bondage and set them free through the blood.

Fast forward to just before Jesus was to be betrayed, arrested, and crucified, when he shared the Passover meal with His disciples. Since the Exodus, it was God's command and Jewish tradition to celebrate the Passover meal, commemorating God's liberation of the children of Israel. Jesus was not the exception to the Passover. The gospels of Matthew, Mark, and Luke tell how Jesus radically changed the meaning and significance of this celebration. Luke 22:19-20 says, "And He took bread, gave thanks and broke it, and gave it to them, saying, "This is My body which is given for you; do this in remembrance of Me." Likewise, He also took the cup after supper, saying, "This cup is the new covenant in My blood, which is shed for you." The Passover meal changed from the Old Covenant to the New Covenant with Jesus. Jesus is the Lamb of God who takes away the sin of the world (John 1:29). The blood of Jesus was shed to set you free, not from Egyptian slavery, but from the penalty and power of sin!

> Just as the blood brought freedom from bondage for the children of Israel, the blood of Jesus breaks your chains into pieces and gives you the freedom that you were created by God to enjoy.

Hebrews 9:22 says, "And according to the law almost all things are purified with blood, and without shedding of blood there is no remission." Your freedom is contingent upon trusting in, receiving, and applying the blood of Jesus to your life. The blood that was applied on the doorposts and lintel by the children of Israel caused God to pass over and not judge. Why? God saw the blood. When you receive the blood of Jesus for the forgiveness of sins and become God's son or daughter, God passes over you and does not condemn or judge you. Why? God sees the blood of

Jesus. The blood of Jesus frees you from the penalty of sin and from the power of sin. Just as the blood brought freedom from bondage for the children of Israel, the blood of Jesus breaks your chains into pieces and gives you the freedom that you were created by God to enjoy.

APPLICATION

WORSHIP:

You can sing and dance before the Lord for freeing you through His blood. Jesus did not need to do this for His sake, but longed to do it for your sake. He loves you! The person who gives pure and extravagant worship is someone who remembers his or her past bondage. Worship comes as natural as breathing to the one who experiences freedom through the cross.

PRAYER:

"Jesus, thank You for giving Your life for me. You died for me. You are so personally involved with my life, and I can't thank You enough for setting me free through Your blood. I honor and worship You; Your blood is powerful and holy. By faith, I apply Your blood to any area that is not free spiritually, emotionally, and physically. Thank You for redeeming me, for purchasing me with Your own life. Your love is transforming. I love You, Jesus, for loving me first. Amen."

DECLARATION:

"I have applied the blood of Jesus to my life. I have all the blessings and benefits (Psalm 103:1-3) that come from the precious blood of Jesus."

ACTION:

Have you received Jesus Christ as your Lord and Savior, by personally putting your trust in the sacrifice He experienced on the cross for you? Have you received Jesus, applying the blood to forgive you? Freedom starts here. If you haven't, take a look at the Introduction to this book again. If you have received Jesus, focus today on what He did on the cross. It was for your freedom that Jesus shed His innocent blood; freedom for your spirit, soul, and body.

DAY 17: FREE FROM THE CURSE

For as many as are of the works of the law are under the curse; for it is written, "Cursed is everyone who does not continue in all things which are written in the book of the law, to do them." But that no one is justified by the law in the sight of God is evident, for "the just shall live by faith." Yet the law is not of faith, but "the man who does them shall live by them." Christ has redeemed us from the curse of the law, having become a curse for us (for it is written, "Cursed is everyone who hangs on a tree"), that the blessing of Abraham might come upon the Gentiles in Christ Jesus, that we might receive the promise of the Spirit through faith (Galatians 3:10-14).

When sin entered the world through Adam, death and destruction followed (Romans 5:12; 6:23). All of the bad news and daily struggles on this earth came from the one act of disobedience to God in the garden of Eden. Naturally, we are all sons and daughters of Adam. Sin spread to the whole human race, and this earth was saturated with sin and all of sin's consequences. The one who has broken the perfect law of God is considered to have sinned, and sin results in the curse of humanity. Everyone who does not perfectly obey God's commands and principles is under the curse. From the curse comes hurt, pain, tears, addictions, fear, anxiety, confusion, disease, poverty, depression, despair, oppression, and any other negative experience.

The powerful truth about the cross that Jesus bled and died on is the fact that He was your substitute. Jesus did not just shed His blood to wipe us clean; Jesus attacked the root of *the curse* that is experienced here on planet earth. Jesus became sin on the cross for you (2 Corinthians 5:21). By becoming sin and taking your punishment for sin on the cross, Jesus overcame sin and death. Since the root of sin was taken care of, the curse that comes from the sin was defeated also! Jesus has secured your freedom from the curse by redeeming, or purchasing, your salvation and freedom through the blood He shed. Galatians 3:13 says, "Christ has redeemed us from the curse of the law, having become a curse for us."

There is no sin, no curse, or no bondage that tries to keep you down and defeated that has power over the blood of Jesus! His blood was poured out for your freedom over the curse of sin. You no longer need to live in defeat to sin. You no longer have to accept fear and anxiety as a part of your life. You no longer have to allow the curse of financial struggle and tormenting disease. You no longer have to be confused and unable to make good and wise decisions. You are no longer broken, bound, or rejected.

> There is no sin, no curse, or no bondage that tries to keep you down and defeated that has power over the blood of Jesus!

Through faith in the blood of Jesus, not only has He taken the curse from you, but He replaced the curse with blessing! Galatians 3:14 tells what happened when Jesus took the curse for you. Jesus added to you where the curse once ruled, dominated, and took from you. Why did He do this? "That the blessing of Abraham might come upon the Gentiles in Christ Jesus, that we might receive the promise of the Spirit through faith." You are mended, healed, whole, forgiven, righteous, a victor, a son and daughter of God, valuable, loved, strong, and full of the presence of God. The curse of sin has been defeated! You are free!

Jesus did all He needed to do to set you free from the curse of sin and death. As Jesus spilled His life-changing blood on the cross, Jesus said, "It is finished" (John 19:30). The work that He accomplished to secure your freedom was finished. Jesus was the all-sufficient sacrifice for all people for all time (Hebrews 7:27).

The question is, what are you doing about it? Do you believe it? Are you trusting in the blood to fully free you from the curse? Is your mind renewed by this truth or are you stuck thinking and believing the lie that nothing will ever change? Think, believe, speak, and then apply the blood of Jesus in your life. Stand strong in this truth. The blood of Jesus never loses.

APPLICATION

WORSHIP:

Thank Jesus for His wonderful grace. He willingly became the curse on the cross so you may have life, eternally and abundantly. Praise Him.

PRAYER:

"Jesus, I apply Your blood to my life by receiving Your finished work for me. I renounce any curse that tries to take a hold of my life in the name of Jesus! I repent and renounce any doors that I have opened through sin and compromise in the name of Jesus! As I shut the door on the lies of the curse, I open my heart and life fully to the blood of Jesus! Thank You, Lord, for cleansing me and setting me free. In Your name, I will think and believe the truth that I am free from the curse of sin and already have the blessings that come from You! I receive it by faith in the name of Jesus. Amen."

DECLARATION:

"I am not cursed. I am fully blessed through the blood of Jesus."

ACTION:

Take note of how you think, speak, and believe when it comes to any of the curses caused by sin. Do you accept your current state because of feelings of unworthiness, insufficiency, or that it must be God's will? What lies are you accepting from the devil that say that you will remain with disease, financial stress, dark habits, and weakness? When you notice these patterns in your life, stand firm in the blood of Jesus that has crushed the curse, and has given you new life!

What curse have you noticed that you may struggle with or is a part of your family history? What seems to torment you and nag you with defeat? Here are 6 action steps to overcome the curse in your life:

1: **Recognize:** Admit and agree with the Word about what is wrong or sinful in your life. Ask the Holy Spirit to reveal any destructive patterns you may struggle with that can be traced back in your family.

2: **Repent:** To repent means that you change your mind about what you do, and hate what is trapping you. At whatever cost, you desire to walk differently.

3: **Renounce:** From your heart and with your mouth, reject and renounce this curse from your life and rebuke it, never to come back into your life. Renounce anything in your life or home that may open the door to temptation or Satan's power and cause you to live by the curse instead of freedom in Christ.

4: **Receive:** Accept God's full acceptance and forgiveness of you. Receive by faith the goodness of the blood of Jesus that crushed the curse.

5: **Renew:** Begin to renew your mind and change the way you think on a daily basis. Do not accept the lie that you are cursed, but stand in God's promises of freedom and blessings that are yours through the blood of Jesus

6: **Revive:** This is the result of applying the blood of Jesus to the curse that tries to steal your freedom; you live again! You are revived back to the life God intended. Now walk in newness of life.

DAY 18: FREE FROM THE DEVIL

And you, being dead in your trespasses and the uncircumcision of your flesh, He has made alive together with Him, having forgiven you all trespasses, having wiped out the handwriting of requirements that was against us, which was contrary to us. And He has taken it out of the way, having nailed it to the cross. Having disarmed principalities and powers, He made a public spectacle of them, triumphing over them in it (Colossians 2:13-15).

You are in a war with spiritual forces of evil that hate you and want you to live in defeat instead of freedom (2 Corinthians 10:3 and Ephesians 6:12). Knowing who we are fighting against is the first step to experiencing freedom, but just knowing a strong enemy has taken advantage of you is not victory. What is important to understand is that the enemy must be weaker before you can win the battle. Even better, when the enemy is disarmed of his weapons he cannot be effective in his attacks.

The incredibly great news is that every demonic force which is trying to keep you bound is, in reality, disarmed. You don't have to take it anymore from the devil because you already have the victory in Christ. The Holy Spirit is with you and in you, and God has equipped you with everything you need to live in freedom in this life (2 Peter 1:3). You are on the winning team and can take the offensive step; every principality and power has no authority over you since they have been disarmed and stripped of authority.

Colossians 2:15 is a powerful verse that speaks of Jesus crushing the devil and every demonic entity that is at war with you. It says that Jesus made a *public spectacle* of them. How ironic that Jesus was humbly suffering on the cross publicly. The people looking on and the demonic forces thought they had defeated and embarrassed Jesus publicly. Yet Jesus openly defeated Satan on the cross for all to see. What seemed like defeat to Jesus in the natural realm was actually a public demonstration of defeat to the devil in the spiritual realm.

This scripture also says that Jesus "triumphed over them in it." The Greek word here is *triambeuo*. The believers in the Colossian church knew exactly what Paul was saying in this language. This is a word to describe the emperor or general coming home from a victory in the enemy's territory or land. It was a triumphant parade upon returning home. The head of the parade was the general or emperor, who would ride into the city on a large, majestic horse. Following the general or emperor were those who fought in the battle. The treasure, weapons, and goods that were taken from the enemy were brought behind all of the military personnel who had fought in battle. Last but not least in the procession, the enemy ruler was paraded for all to see. He was clearly beaten and bound for all to watch and enjoy his defeat. This is what is meant when Jesus triumphed over the devil; the devil has been humiliated at the cross!

Jesus boldly and confidently defeated Satan on the cross. His victory is our victory. Christ stripped the authority and power of the devil and his cohorts on the cross, and has given us the victory and authority over the devil. The enemy is bound and beat. We have much to rejoice over!

A young man shared a powerful testimony with me once. As a youth pastor, I used to plan a service with other youth pastors in the community that was geared toward teenagers. One particular night the guest minister was calling youth to come forward, and many flooded the altar. The other youth ministers and I laid ours hands on the teenagers to minister to them, praying for them as they surrendered their lives to the Lord Jesus. Later that same year, my wife and I went to a nearby church to hear an evangelist we personally knew. As we sat in the seat before service, a young man who was sitting behind me tapped my shoulder and said, "Do you remember me?" I was honest and said that he didn't look familiar to me. He went on to say that he heard of the youth service that we had earlier in the year. He said that he was a Satanist and had gone to the service to pray against it while he sat in the sanctuary. He went on to explain that he had been training to become a Satanic priest and had experienced numerous spiritual wonders. Then he said that in spite of his efforts to attack the work of God that night, God had worked on him. When the call came to respond to Jesus, he found himself responding and went to the altar. Little did I know that I had prayed over him that night and he surrendered his life to Jesus! His countenance was full of joy as he shared that God not only changed him, but called him to the ministry. Praise the Lord!

Christ stripped the authority and power of the devil and his cohorts on the cross, and has given us the victory and authority over the devil.

How silly it is to struggle, give the devil credit for our misery, cower in following Jesus, and strive to get victory. This amazing truth needs to sink deep into your heart: Satan is already defeated! Reject his lies! He is bound and beat through the blood of Jesus. Stand up and take your territory back. Freedom is yours in the powerful blood of Jesus. Take authority and live in the victory that has already been won!

Now thanks be to God who always leads us in triumph (*triambeuo*) in Christ (2 Corinthians 2:14).

APPLICATION

WORSHIP:
Think of Jesus rising from the dead, "riding His horse" in the parade of victory. Worship God for His love for you that He went

to the cross, securing your victory. Worship and sing praises loud and with great celebration!

PRAYER:

"Jesus, thank You for making a public spectacle of Satan! I love that You have saved me and set me free. I now understand that my enemy and those things which try to keep me bound are actually defeated and have been disarmed. I rest in the work of the cross over Satan and live in freedom. Satan has been stripped of authority, and I have authority in You. Thank You, Jesus!"

DECLARATION:

"I have overcome the accuser of my life by the blood of the Lamb and the word of my testimony" (Revelation 12:11).

ACTION:

Renew your mind. Read and meditate on Colossians 2:15 over and over with the knowledge of what the Holy Spirit is saying. Jesus has won the battle for you already. Walk in it and rejoice in Jesus who is your victory.

DAY 19: FREE FROM SICKNESS

Surely He has borne our griefs and carried our sorrows; yet we esteemed Him stricken, smitten by God, and afflicted. But He was wounded for our transgressions, He was bruised for our iniquities; the chastisement for our peace was upon Him, and by His stripes we are healed (Isaiah 53:4-5).

When evening had come, they brought to Him many who were demon-possessed. And He cast out the spirits with a word, and healed all who were sick, that it might be fulfilled which was spoken by Isaiah the prophet, saying: "He Himself took our infirmities and bore our sicknesses" (Matthew 8:16-17).

When Jesus bled for you on the cross, He not only made a way to remove your sin, but His blood was the ultimate provision for your healing. It is the nature of God to heal. In fact, God revealed himself in Exodus 15:26 as Jehovah Rapha, which is "I am the Lord your Physician, the Lord who heals you." You cannot separate healing from God, for it is His name, His nature. A healer heals; God heals because He is a healer. Sickness is part of the curse of sin on the earth. Jesus paid for sin and the curse of sin on the cross. He died a tortuous death and paid, or redeemed you, from your sickness. You do not have to carry your sickness because Jesus carried it for you.

The prophet Isaiah had foreseen Jesus suffering on the cross and declared the power of the blood of Jesus. Isaiah explains in chapter 53:4-

5 what the blood of Jesus did for you. Jesus died for *your* sickness, *your* pains, *your* transgressions, *your* iniquities, *your* peace, and *your* healing. The apostle Peter declared this truth by explaining that Jesus bore our sins and healed our sickness on the cross. He states that we *were* healed (1 Peter 2:24).

You may say, "Did Isaiah really prophesy about Jesus' blood defeating sickness? I thought it was just about our sin." The answer to your question is found in the text. Jesus literally carried our sickness and pain on the cross. Since sin is the root of sickness and part of the curse, and Jesus paid for sin, then sickness is included. Isaiah says that by the stripes of Jesus, or His wounds caused by being scourged and nailed to the cross, healing flowed to all that come to Him.

Matthew quotes Isaiah 53:4 when he witnessed Jesus casting out demons and healing *all* who were sick (Matthew 8:16-17). Forgiveness of sins as well as the healing of the body are the blessings and benefits that you receive through the blood of Jesus (Psalm 103:1-3). The love and compassion of Jesus is His motive for healing your body. He was compassionate toward the leper, the multitude, and the blind (Mark 1:40-45; Matthew 14:13-14; 20:29-34).

"Jesus Christ is the same yesterday, today, and forever" (Hebrews 13:8). He has not changed in His love for you or His power toward you. He provided all that you need as the sacrificial Lamb who bled to death on the cross.

You don't earn or deserve healing—it is a free gift. Healing comes by God's grace.

Here is the question: Have you put your faith in the blood of Jesus for healing, just like you did for salvation and forgiveness of sin? Have you believed what the Bible says about healing through the blood of Jesus, or is your faith in your natural circumstances, feelings, and symptoms? Have you thanked God for shedding His blood for your healing and restoration?

Are you believing the lie of Satan that says that sickness will prevail, or have you applied the blood for your healing?

God goes to great lengths in His Word to communicate to mankind that it is His will to heal, especially by going to the cross. His kingdom has no sickness. Our prayer and call to God is that His kingdom come and rule our life, and His will be done as His will is done in heaven (Matthew 6:10). You will never be free from sickness until you believe and act on the truth that the blood of Jesus was not spilled in vain, but heals you. You don't earn or deserve healing—it is a free gift. Healing comes by God's grace. His grace was shed for you at Calvary. Your part is to receive the free gift of healing; apply the blood of Jesus, and praise Him for the power of healing through His blood. Sickness and disease must disappear in the presence of the blood of Jesus.

APPLICATION

WORSHIP:

Begin to thank Jesus for His blood that has healed you. In the midst of your pain and disease, worship Jesus for healing you. Worshipping God and thanking Him before you see the manifestation of what He has promised is using your eyes of faith. Worship Jesus for His work on the cross.

PRAYER:

"Jesus, thank You for willingly taking my sickness and disease on the cross. When the Father poured His wrath and judgement on You for my sin, He also poured His wrath on my sickness and disease that You bore. I reject any lie that healing is not mine; I rebuke your lies Satan. I believe Your work and put my faith in Your blood, Jesus. I believe that I receive healing in Jesus' name. Amen."

DECLARATION:

"By His stripes, I am healed" (Isaiah 53:5).

ACTION:

Healing is the will of God. God is not just able to do it, His provision comes through the blood of Jesus. His blood has healing power for you. God does not pick and choose who to heal. The cross is for the whole world, for full and complete forgiveness, and full and complete healing. God is willing. He wants to heal you because He already died for your sickness. Reach out, believe this truth, and apply the blood of Jesus daily until you see the healing take place. Rejoice on His promise of healing through His Word. Receive and believe on His Word. Let this promise saturate your mind all day long until it is grounded in your heart and mind: "He sent His word and healed them" (Psalm 107:20).

DAY 20: THE DNA OF GOD

Knowing that you were not redeemed with corruptible things, like silver or gold, from your aimless conduct received by tradition from your fathers, but with the precious blood of Christ, as of a lamb without blemish and without spot.... having been born again, not of corruptible seed but incorruptible, through the word of God which lives and abides forever (1 Peter 1:18-19, 23).

Simon Peter, a bondservant and apostle of Jesus Christ, to those who have obtained like precious faith with us by the righteousness of our God and Savior Jesus Christ: Grace and peace be multiplied to you in the knowledge of God and of Jesus our Lord, as His divine power has given to us all things that pertain to life and godliness, through the knowledge of Him who called us by glory and virtue, by which have been given to us exceedingly great and precious promises, that through these you may be partakers of the divine nature, having escaped the corruption that is in the world through lust (2 Peter 1:1-4).

When God created you, He placed DNA within you. Without getting too scientific, your DNA is basically the carrier of your genetic information. It is the hereditary material that makes you who you are—your fundamental and unique characteristics and qualities. Your DNA was in you when He formed you in your mother's womb (Psalm 139:13 ESV) and is present in all of your cells, which make up who you are by nature. Much of your DNA is found in your blood, specifically in your white blood cells. The genetic information that dictates who you are (your skin color, your smile, how you walk, what your hands look like, etc.) was passed down to you from your mother and father. You have probably heard comments from family members that compare you to other family members saying, "It's in the genes. You look or act like such and such family member."

When God created mankind, He created man and woman in His own image. He created mankind in perfection and said it was good (Genesis 1:26-31). When Adam and Eve sinned, the earth was cursed with death and destruction. The perfect nature of man was contaminated with sin and caused mankind to be broken and bound in the ways of thinking, of feeling negative emotions, of hurting others and being hurt, of suffering with disease, and experiencing the consequences of death and destruction. Man's nature was changed by one man's offense (Romans 5:12).

Jesus came to destroy the curse of sin and death by becoming sin on the cross, so anyone who puts their faith in Jesus receives His righteousness (2 Corinthians 5:21). It is a beautiful exchange that happens because of the blood of Jesus. He is referred to as the second Adam, because just as sin spread to all of humanity through Adam's initial act of disobedience, so the righteousness of God is spread to anyone that puts their faith in the obedient act of Christ's work on the cross (Romans 5:15-19).

In Christ, now you have new DNA, and it was inherited when you accepted the life-changing power of the blood of Jesus.

When you trusted in the blood of Jesus and received Jesus, you changed. You have been born again! Your identity—or who you are—is now in Christ. You are now a new creation; the old has passed away (2 Corinthians 5:17). God has completely changed your destiny because now you have a new nature. Before believing in and receiving Jesus, your nature was rebellion, sin, and disobedience to God (Ephesians 2:3). But in Christ, now you have new DNA, and it was inherited when you accepted the life-changing power of the blood of Jesus. Your characteristics and qualities have completely changed. You are now a partaker of God's divine nature (2 Peter 1:4). Since trusting in Christ, God lives in you through the Holy Spirit; you are now the residing place, or temple, of God (1 Corinthians 3:16). You now have the DNA of God through the transformation of the blood of Jesus; it has saved you, healed you, redeemed you, delivered you, and has completely set you free.

Applying the blood of Jesus to your life changes everything. Without knowing the truth of who you are in Christ and knowing that you now have His nature, you will never be completely free because you will always struggle trying to live from your old nature. The old nature died and was buried with Christ; He rose again so you can live in victory with the nature of God (Romans 6:4). Your old nature is not in the process of dying; it is dead! Know your God-given DNA through the blood of Jesus. Live as who you really are and you will never be the same. Live in freedom, son or daughter of God!

APPLICATION

WORSHIP:

It is out of your changed nature that you can worship the Lord in spirit and in truth. Worship Him out of being completely changed, set free, and transformed by His life-changing blood.

PRAYER:

"Lord, I am forever grateful that You shed Your blood for the whole world, and am thankful that You did it for *me*. I accept fully Your truth that I am new. You have broken my chains and destroyed the bondage in my life. Your blood is precious and life-changing. Help me to live as who I am in You. I have Your nature now and am able to do exceedingly abundantly above all because of Your presence in me."

DECLARATION:

"God has changed my DNA through the blood of Jesus; I have the nature of God" (2 Peter 1:4).

ACTION:

You are halfway there today. The truth of the Word that declares *what you have* and *who you are,* are crucial to know, believe, accept, and put into action. For more information about your new nature, read the book of Ephesians. Do you hear the chains falling? You are becoming who you are. You are free. Be empowered today to walk in freedom!

PART V: BELIEVE

Put Your Faith in God

DAY 21: FREEDOM BY FAITH

Now faith is the substance of things hoped for, the evidence of things not seen (Hebrews 11:1).

Freedom without faith is impossible. The apostle John said that it is our faith that overcomes the world (1 John 5:4). When the Word of God speaks about faith, it is not talking about a religious system, but believing, trusting, and personally depending on God and His Word. Faith is trusting in what God says just because of who God is. Because God is holy and perfect, what He says is always true. God's Word is trustworthy. Because God Himself is trustworthy, His nature and character fully back up what He says. God is faithful to His promise. Therefore, faith is believing what God says and counting it as already done.

Faith is the eyesight of God. When you believe what God says, you come into alignment with His will, His heart, and His purposes. Faith is choosing to see life from God's perspective rather than from this world's perspective. It understands that the unseen world existed before the natural world, and that God's kingdom rules over the natural kingdom. Faith is the evidence of things not seen (Hebrews 11:1-3). When you put your faith in what God says and who He is, it doesn't matter how big the mountain is in front of you, it will move because you take God at His word (Mark 11:22-24).

Faith in God and His Word frees you because it lifts you up into the realm of the kingdom of God. The opposite of faith is doubt, and doubt ties you up with chains that bring you to the land of hopelessness and despair. Faith is what unlocks the door to God's best and blessings; it gives you access to God and is the way to apply all of God's benefits in your life. Faith opens up the door to salvation, forgiveness, healing, deliverance, peace, restoration, boldness and confidence, financial blessing, strength, and complete wholeness.

Faith fully accepts what God says and is confident in His promises. The word *faith* literally means "firm persuasion, assurance, and a guarantee." When Jesus walked this earth, lived life with His disciples, taught the multitudes, and ministered to those He touched, He taught who He was. His mission was to reveal His nature so all of mankind can know Him. Once you know Jesus, His purpose is to teach you to put faith in Him. The truth is that it is hard to have faith in someone you do not know. God's desire is for you to know Jesus, and as you know Him, you believe and trust in what He says. Then—and only then—will you have confidence and peace.

> ## Faith opens up the door to salvation, forgiveness, healing, deliverance, peace, restoration, boldness and confidence, financial blessing, strength, and complete wholeness.

What is it that has kept you trapped? Is there any doubt about your freedom? Do you truly and wholly believe that God can and will do the impossible in your situation? It is time to rise up with great faith in what God says and reveals in His Word. Believe with your whole heart. Do not be tempted to doubt. God's nature and God's Word never changes. God is trustworthy, and His Word is always reliable. You have faith, and your faith will be perfected by Jesus (Hebrews 12:2 ESV). Make a choice today and live by faith (Romans 1:17). Your freedom is found as you live by faith and not by sight (2 Corinthians 5:7).

APPLICATION

WORSHIP:

As you believe in God and His Word, you will grow close to Him as He acts according to your faith in what He says. The man who was healed by Jesus in John chapter 9 said, "Lord, I believe!" And then he worshiped Jesus (John 9:38). We should do this too. Worship Him as you have faith in God and His Word.

PRAYER:

"Jesus, thank You for loving me enough to come to me and save me. By your grace and through my faith in You, I know You. Knowing You is the greatest thing in my life; You have changed my life! I renew my faith and trust in Your Word today. Help me not to doubt but to always believe what You say. In Jesus' name. Amen."

DECLARATION:

"My victory that makes me an overcomer is my faith in God and His Word!" (1 John 5:4).

ACTION:

What are you doubting? What doesn't make sense? Replace the doubt with faith according to the Word of God. Make this the theme of your life: "It's according to the Word of God."

DAY 22: SUSTAINING FAITH

> Therefore we do not lose heart. Even though our outward man is perishing, yet the inward man is being renewed day by day. For our light affliction, which is but for a moment, is working for us a far more exceeding and eternal weight of glory, while we do not look at the things which are seen, but at the things which are not seen. For the things which are seen are temporary, but the things which are not seen are eternal....For we walk by faith, not by sight (2 Corinthians 4:16-18, 5:7).

Faith believes what God says and what God promises—no matter what. It sees through the infinite eyes of God rather than through our limited eyes and understanding.

More times than not, the enemy will start to speak his lies in your face by bringing up two circumstances that can quench your fire of faith, but only if you accept it. The first mistake is to rely on our natural senses while believing God for His promise. Many do not see, feel, smell, hear, or taste what God said He would do. The symptoms in the body look and feel sick. You hear the consistency of the bad news all around you. The mountain that is before you looks bigger than ever and there seem to be no answers. Since there isn't any evidence of what you prayed and believed for, there must be a problem; either you must not deserve it or God must not want to do the miracle. You begin to think that God doesn't care and He hasn't heard your cry. Doubt and discouragement set in because you don't see the manifestation or fulfillment of what God's Word says, and before long you give up. Faith is short-lived and you go by what you see, hear, feel, smell, and taste. Since the natural is what is real to you, your faith wavers and God's promise is set to the side.

Another big mistake people make when believing God is relying on time. You have been believing God for your freedom. You believe He healed you on the cross; you believe Jesus took your guilt and shame away; you believe that the Holy Spirit has empowered you for life and godliness; and you have put your faith in what God says about meeting your material and financial needs. You believe, but only on your terms and your time. When you don't see *immediate* results, discouragement sets in and you begin to doubt whether God said anything to you or not. What began in faith ends in doubt because it didn't happen right away. When the devil knows that you are downcast over not seeing the promise fulfilled, he will condemn you by telling you that your faith is weak and powerless. He will say, "If you believed enough, God would have answered quickly. God let you down. Don't trust in His Word; you are made to suffer and put up with your situation. You can't trust God." This is a Satanic trap.

Great faith believes God, even before there is change—even when the fulfillment to the promise is not yet evident in the natural.

Great faith believes God, even before there is change—even when the fulfillment to the promise is not yet evident in the natural. When you pray to God and speak His Word, put your faith in what God says. Sometimes God fulfills His promises immediately; other times, the fulfillment to the promise takes time. Whether it is immediate or done in the future, God never lies and He can be trusted. God's will is for you to believe Him at His word, and keep on believing in His promises to you, not because you see it in the natural, but because your faithful and trustworthy God said it. This is when your *overcoming* faith is connected to your *sustaining* faith. You believe in the promise based on God alone. God said it, period. That is all you need to believe.

Noah believed God when He told him to build an ark because something called rain would come and flood the earth. The flood did not happen as soon as Noah believed, but he continued in faith (Hebrews 11:7). Abraham was promised a son even when he was childless in an old age. God did not manifest the promise immediately, yet at the appointed time, Isaac was born (Hebrews 11:11-12). When God promised Joshua that He would give him the city of Jericho and told him to march around the walls of the city, the walls didn't fall immediately. Joshua believed the word of God and had to continue to believe each day as he obeyed. The walls eventually fell, just as God promised (Joshua 6:1-27).

The Lord has taught me this principle of faith in so many ways, and I know He will continue to do so, but one experience caused my wife and I to put sustaining faith into high gear. We had been married for a couple of years and wanted to start a family together, but it wasn't happening. We went to the doctor, and words came out of the doctor's mouth that were not what we wanted to hear, "You will never have children." The doctor proceeded to say that he had medical alternatives, but it would be a waste of time. He said that it was probably not going to happen. With that said, we went to the Lord.

God spoke clearly to my wife, telling her that we shouldn't go through any medical alternatives to help with the possibility of getting pregnant, but to trust in Him and His unchanging power and promises to heal. I was in full agreement, so we waited. One year later, nothing. Two years, nothing. Three years had gone by, and the doctor still confirmed that it was not possible. Do you know what happened after four years? Nothing still. The years got rough. We held on to what God said, but it was not always easy to believe what God said to us, especially when we didn't see or feel it as time moved forward without getting the miracle. I got to the point where I asked my wife, "Are you sure you don't want to try something that the doctor would give?" I remember her looking at me with a look that said, "I'm desperate and long to have a child, but no—God said He will do it." Her faith inspired me, and we renewed our trust in the Lord.

Finally, the fifth year of waiting proved to be the year when God did what He promised us and spoke specifically to us. My wife was pregnant with our miracle child! We were ecstatic and praised our God for being so faithful to His promises. The best part is that even today we share this amazing story of healing and trust in God. All glory goes to Him because the miracle did not happen in our timing, but God fulfilled what He said to us and did the miracle! We had faith, but it was *sustaining* faith. God gave us His grace during this process to continue in faith in His unchanging nature and words. Five years after our miracle son was born, God was so good that He gave us a second son, another miracle. God is faithful!

Put your faith in what God has said, even when it looks like nothing is happening and His promise hasn't manifested yet. As you set your eyes on God's promise, your faith will sustain you and cause great victory as you trust in Him! God is always faithful to what He promises you. Keep the faith; your breakthrough is coming!

APPLICATION

WORSHIP:

Thank God before you see the promise fulfilled. Worship God because your freedom and answered prayer has already been set in the realm of the kingdom of God. Worship the Lord because you have what He has promised, even before it is fulfilled in the natural.

PRAYER:

"Lord, my God, though I may not see any answers in my body, my finances, my relationship, or in my _____, I believe that You will do what You promised. No matter what I see or what time it takes, my faith is grounded in You. I receive your promise and believe by seeing through Your eyes until I see it with my natural eyes. Promise of God, come forth in Jesus' name! Amen!"

DECLARATION:

"I walk by faith, not by sight!" (2 Corinthians 5:7).

ACTION:

In what areas of your life has the devil discouraged you and brought about doubt in your mind? What are you depending on in the natural? What timetable have you believed that authorizes your ability to remain in faith? Choose today to believe in God's Word. No matter what you see or feel, and no matter how long it may be, trust in Jesus. He is trustworthy and will never lie. Grow in your sustaining faith!

DAY 23: FAITH PLEASES GOD

But without faith it is impossible to please Him, for he who comes to God must believe that He is, and that He is a rewarder of those who diligently seek Him (Hebrews 11:6).

When you put your trust and faith in God and His Word, it pleases the Lord. Today's passage says, "But without faith, it is impossible to please Him" (Hebrews 11:6). A couple of truths that this scripture reveals must be thought through. First of all, if faith pleases God, and your desire is to please the Lord, then you must understand how to have faith that pleases Him. Secondly, why does faith please God anyway? When faith is absent, why is God not pleased?

Perhaps you have read this verse a number of times, but tend to steer away from it because the father of lies, the devil, has condemned you by speaking to you about how you struggle to believe. You may feel that you don't please God because you don't have enough faith to do great things. The truth that you must receive is that Jesus is the Author and Finisher of your faith (Hebrews 12:2). He has given you a measure of faith by His great love and grace so you can believe in Him (Romans 12:3). In fact, Jesus said that if you even have faith as small as a mustard seed you can speak to the mountain in your life and it will move (Matthew 17:20). The kind of faith that the author of Hebrews is talking about is the faith in God that you start with. You have put your faith in the Lord, knowing that He first exists, and that He will reward you as you diligently seek Him (Hebrews 11:6).

Does God call you to grow in your faith and trust in Him and His Word? Absolutely! But that doesn't mean that God isn't pleased with you because of the size of your faith right now. Reject the condemnation from the accuser and receive the good news that Jesus has given you faith to trust in Him. Putting your faith in Jesus and seeking Him is faith that pleases God. Rejoice in the faith you do have, but understand that God desires that you do not stay stagnant in your level of faith either. He gives you faith so that it will grow and increase. Jesus gives you a measure of faith, but it is your responsibility to grow your faith in Him and the Word of God.

Faith pleases God because God is pleased with blessing you, and faith is what receives what He promises.

Why is God pleased with your faith in Him? The answer is so exciting and powerful! When you put your faith and trust in Jesus, it unlocks the door to knowing God and receiving all that God has provided for you and desires to give to you. God has already provided all you need: salvation, healing, deliverance, peace, and so on. Faith is seeing what God has given to you and reaching out to receive it. When you believe God's promises, you receive from God. Faith pleases God so much because He is a rewarder! Faith pleases God because God loves to fill you, bless you, free you, and do more than you can ever think or imagine! (Ephesians 3:20) Since faith is the invitation and acceptance of what God wants to do in your life and through your life, God is pleased when you operate in faith so He can make you prosper in all your ways. You cannot please God apart from faith because faith receives the reward, and God is a loving Father who loves to give and reward! So faith pleases God because God is pleased with blessing you, and faith is what receives what He promises.

Believe in the promises of God for your own life today. Knowing your loving and generous God, be diligent to seek Him and surrender to Him. Your faith in who He is and what He says pleases Him greatly, for God is a rewarder and is waiting to fulfill what He has promised in His Word for your life.

Faith and trust in someone is necessary for a healthy relationship. Trust your Father; believe His Word. Allow Him to work mightily in your life as you have faith and trust in Him. Experience freedom in Christ through faith.

APPLICATION

WORSHIP:

Honor God and magnify Him for who He is. Sing from your heart and with faith for who He is and thank Him for what He has done.

PRAYER:

"Lord, I believe what You say in Your Word and I trust You. I am so thankful to serve such a wonderful God. I know You are grieved when I do not believe, because it keeps Your best from being fulfilled in my life. Thank You for revealing to me how You are a rewarder and a generous giver. I receive You, Your Word, and all its blessings that are promised to me today by faith. I trust You. In Jesus' name. Amen."

DECLARATION:

"I am rewarded and blessed because I have faith in God!" (Hebrews 11:6).

ACTION:

Faith knows what God says will come to pass. Today, think about anything that is hindering your faith. Is there something you are reading that causes doubt to arise? Perhaps there is a person you need to break ties with because their consistent negativity and doubt about God and His Word is discouraging you. Even what you watch or listen to can hinder your faith, especially if it is against God's truth. Do whatever it takes to help you trust and believe what God says to you. You will not be disappointed!

DAY 24: STEPS OF FAITH

And he received the sign of circumcision, a seal of the righteousness of the faith which he had while still uncircumcised, that he might be the father of all those who believe, though they are uncircumcised, that righteousness might be imputed to them also, and the father of circumcision to those who not only are of the circumcision, but who also walk in the *steps of the faith* which our father Abraham had while still uncircumcised (Romans 4:11-12).

It is crucial to know that faith in God and faith in His Word is what pleases God because it opens the door for Him to pour out the blessings of what He has already promised for your life. It is also important to understand that it is necessary to continue to walk forward in faith. As you journey through this life on earth you will continually take steps of faith based on what God is saying to you through His Word and where the Holy Spirit is leading you to walk.

Today's scripture shows how Abraham took steps of faith at certain times and moments in his life. Abraham had to make a choice whether to believe what was familiar and natural, or to believe what God said. Abraham's faith in God and his relationship with God grew as he took steps that were ordered by Him. The same is true for you.

Believing God just because God said something is stubborn faith that does not move away from God or His promises for you. As you take the steps of faith, you will find that each step will remove anything in your life that is keeping you bound, and you will experience amazing freedom by holding on to faith in what God is saying to you.

In order to take *steps* of faith, you must know the *stages* of faith. The scriptures talk about having no faith, little faith, great faith, and perfect faith. Each stage of faith has a voice, and that voice is actually what you are speaking to yourself and to God as you are faced with a choice and each step.

Having *no faith* is unbelief, which *says that God can not and will not.* The Bible says that those who do not believe forfeit much, from knowing God and being saved, to experiencing the miracles that God desires to do. Those who were familiar with Jesus as a carpenter in his hometown of Nazareth rejected Jesus as the Messiah and Savior. Jesus wanted to do many wonderful works at home, but He was not able to because of the people's unbelief (Matthew 13:58). Without faith, your freedom will be hindered.

Each stage of faith has a voice, and that voice is actually what you are speaking to yourself and to God as you are faced with a choice and each step.

Little faith says God *can* do it, but you're *not sure if He will* do it. Little faith is a recipe which includes both faith and doubt. It believes God *can* do something, but does not have complete assurance. When Jesus walked on water, Peter had faith to have Jesus call him out to do the same. Peter took a step and walked on water, but when he saw (seeing in the natural) the wind and waves around him, he began to fear and started sinking. Jesus immediately caught Peter with His hand and said, "O you of *little faith*, why did you doubt?" (Matthew 14:31).

Great faith says God *can and will* do it. It not only believes that God has the power to do what He promised, but that God has perfect love and mercy to do what He says. Great faith believes that God has the ability *and* the desire. A centurion came to Jesus in faith. His servant was ill, dreadfully tormented, and lying at home paralyzed. Jesus promised the centurion that He would heal him, but in humility, the centurion told Jesus to just declare a word and his servant would be healed right where he was at home. The centurion had great faith; he believed Jesus had the power and willingness to heal the servant. Jesus said, "Assuredly I say to you, I have not found such *great faith,* not even in Israel!*"* (Matthew 8:10).

Perfect faith says *it has already been done.* When you have perfect faith, you are fully confident in what God has already promised. You have perfect peace and rest in your heart and mind. The way you see it, if God said it, it has already been accomplished. It's more than believing that God is able and willing to do something for you in the future; you know it is already finished. Abraham fully believed in God's promise of making him a father of many nations. Romans 4:20-21 says of Abraham, "He did not waver at the promise of God through unbelief, but was strengthened in faith, giving glory to God, and being fully convinced that what He had promised He was also able to perform." This great work *was* already performed by God, his part was to believe it to be so.

What are you believing God for as you move forward in freedom? Be fully convinced with your eyes of faith. See what God sees. Believe that what God says has already been accomplished. Step into perfect faith, and you will begin to see with your natural eyes what you first saw with your eyes of faith.

APPLICATION

WORSHIP:
Thank God for His promise. Begin to sing praises to Him. As you worship Him, focus on His faithfulness. He has set you free already (Romans 6:18). Worship Him and choose to have perfect faith which says, "God has promised, so it is done!"

PRAYER:
"Jesus, help any area of unbelief in me. I pray as in Mark 9:24, "I do believe, but help me overcome my unbelief!" I pray that I will become a person who has perfect faith. As I walk with You, I want to know You and believe that what You have said is already done. I put my faith in You and know that what You have promised

for me in Your Word has been done. I align my life under your promises. You have blessed me beyond measure. As I pray, I believe that I have what You already promised (Mark 11:24). In Jesus' name, Amen."

DECLARATION:

"I believe that I have already received what God has promised!" (Mark 11:24).

ACTION:

As you are taking steps of faith, what stage of faith are you in? Are there any areas of unbelief, little faith, great faith, or perfect faith? Take inventory of what you say about areas of your life in which you are needing freedom, healing, and wholeness. Ask the Lord to increase your faith. By God's grace toward you, He will enable you to perfect your faith. After all, Jesus is not only the source, but perfecter of your faith (Hebrews 12:2).

DAY 25: INCREASING FAITH

So then faith comes by hearing, and hearing by the word of God (Romans 10:17).

Chances are, after seeing the great blessing and rewards of having great faith and perfect faith, and knowing what stage you are in when it comes to your own faith in God's Word, you most likely desire to increase in faith. You are certainly not alone! The disciples heard the teachings of Jesus and saw the great works of God because of faith. This caused them to ask Jesus to increase their faith (Luke 17:5).

This request to increase faith was apparently true. In Mark 9:14-29, a father brought his son who was possessed by a demon to Jesus. The evil spirit made the boy mute, threw him down to the ground, caused him to foam at the mouth, and made him gnash his teeth. The father explained how he brought his son to the disciples and they could not cast the demon out. Jesus rebuked the disciples' unbelief. Jesus went on to explain that if you can believe, all things are possible. The father then said, "Lord, I believe; help my unbelief" (Mark 9:24). This shows that faith can increase, and it is the will of God to increase your faith. The disciples needed to increase their faith, and this father desired for his own faith to increase. The good news? If Jesus commands you to believe, then it is possible to increase your faith.

Faith increases through hearing God's Word. Romans 10:17 says that faith comes by hearing. Hearing what? Hearing the Word of God. You need to have ears that are ready to hear from God. Each morning when you wake up it is important to purposefully and intentionally surrender your heart to God and ask the Holy Spirit to keep your heart ready to receive from God and willing to listen to His voice throughout the day. Ask the Holy Spirit to keep your heart soft and your ears sensitive to God's voice. Listening to God's Word is what will increase your faith. This means that God's Word must be priority in your life. The more you hear God's Word in your life, the more you will believe and receive what God says. Faith comes through God's Word because you hear God's voice and see how God moved in the lives of many who have gone before you; both of these things will build your faith.

Faith increases when you ask God. The Lord loves when you ask Him to increase your faith. It is a prayer He will answer because it is His will. Asking God to increase your faith shows Him that you are focused on Him, you desire to live in accordance with the kingdom of God, and that you want to please Him. Even the disciples were told by Jesus they did not have the faith to cast the demon out of the father's son. He said that they needed to pray and fast (Mark 9:28-29). This would help purge out unbelief in their lives and build faith to believe the next time they minister like this again. Spending time alone with God, knowing Him, asking Him for help, and listening to His Word will increase your faith.

> Asking God to increase your faith shows Him that you are focused on Him, you desire to live in accordance with the kingdom of God, and that you want to please Him.

Faith increases when you get close to those who are close with God. When you begin to hear what God is doing in another's life, your faith increases. This is because you are not only hearing the Word of God through others, but you are actually hearing and seeing God work personally and powerfully in others' lives. You see God as active and ready to do what He promised already. Be aware that you will become like the people you are close to. Find godly relationships, those in the local church who you can get to know and do life with.

Building relationships where God is at the center will encourage you and help increase your faith. The disciples' faith grew because they lived life with Jesus and received all that He desired in their lives. Their faith also grew because they were in each other's company, consistently urging each other on.

Be encouraged today. If you lack faith, know that God loves you and knows your heart. He is committed to you; God is faithful even when you lack faith (2 Timothy 2:13). Believe in Jesus and His promise. You will experience wonderful freedom when you fully believe in who God is and what He says. Freedom increases as your faith increases.

APPLICATION

WORSHIP:

When you worship and focus on the greatness of God, you will notice that your faith arises. The reason is that you see Him, and nothing compares to His great power and majesty.

PRAYER:

"Lord, I put my whole trust in You. Increase my faith. I desire You and all that You have promised, and I receive it all by faith. Help me become a person who has perfect faith, complete assurance that what I pray for has already happened. Thank You for Your love for me and commitment to help my faith increase. Amen."

DECLARATION:

"I believe all things are possible!" (Mark 9:23).

ACTION:

Saturate your mind with hearing God's Word. Remove anything from your life that is contrary to the truth. In prayer, believe God is increasing your faith. Be intentional about getting close to those close with God. Watch how your faith increases and true freedom is found as increased faith replaces doubt.

PART VI: OBEY

Follow God

DAY 26: FAITH
CONFIRMED

> But someone will say, "You have faith, and I have works." Show me your faith without your works, and I will show you my faith by my works.... For as the body without the spirit is dead, so faith without works is dead also (James 2:18, 26).

The freedom that God has provided for you is real and life-changing. Removing any ounce of unbelief and abandoning yourself fully to God by believing His Word will catapult you to victory. Faith in who God is and what He has said is absolutely necessary if you desire to experience freedom in your spirit, soul (mind and emotions), and body. James speaks about this type of faith in James 2:14-26. Genuine faith does not only include believing in your heart that God has already accomplished what He has promised, but it also includes obedience. In fact, God says that obedience to what He commands and calls you to is the true sign that you have fully believed God.

I can believe all I want that if I turn the light switch to the *on* position that the lights will go on, but if I never actually turn it on, it will reveal a couple of truths. First, the light won't go on. I will not enjoy the benefits of taking action on what I believe. Second, it will cause others not to believe what I say I believe. They will hear my mouth declaring that I believe turning the light switch on will cause the light to come on. I will be declaring what I believe, but they will doubt my faith because I never act on it.

God called Noah to build an ark because He was going to flood the earth. Noah believed what God said (Genesis 6:13-14) and built an ark (Genesis 6:22). God promised Abraham He'd provide a land with great blessings and that he would be a father of many nations. Abraham believed God and he departed from the land he was told to leave and became the father of many (Genesis 12:1-3). God told Moses that He would not strike the firstborn of anyone who sacrificed the lamb and applied the blood on the doorposts and lintel of the home. Moses believed, and he and the children of Israel applied the blood (Exodus 12). God promised the city of Jericho to Joshua and commanded him to march around the city seven times. Joshua believed, and they marched (Joshua 6). Jesus anointed the blind man with clay mixed with His saliva. He told the blind man to go wash in the pool of Siloam. The blind man believed because he obeyed Jesus by washing, and he was healed (John 9:6-7). James 2:18 says, "I will show you my faith by my works." Works do not take the place of faith in God's promises, but it shows that you believe God and His words. Works are the proof of your faith.

> Genuine faith does not only include believing in your heart that God has already accomplished what He has promised, but it also includes obedience.

Jesus was preaching in a house. Crowds gathered to hear Him speak words of life. It was so crowded that there was no more room either inside or outside of the house. People pressed to hear Jesus. A paralytic man and his friends believed that Jesus was the Healer, but the crowd was so numerous that they could not get into the house. So they went up to the roof to make a way in. The friends lowered the paralytic, who was lying on the bed, right down into the house—right in front of Jesus. The scripture says, "When Jesus **saw** their faith" (Mark 2:5). Jesus told the man that his sins were forgiven and healed him physically. There was substance to their faith! Their faith and dependence on Jesus as the healer was evident by coming to Him, even if it meant making a hole in the roof and lowering the sick man down. Their faith was seen through action. Faith was shown by obedience.

Whatever you need freedom from, your confident faith in Jesus and believing what He says working alongside obedience and action will cause great victory and blessings to flow in your life. Prove your faith with obedience. The promise of God will be yours!

APPLICATION

WORSHIP:

Obedience to God is worship. As you sing to Him, offer your life before Him and commit yourself to obey what you believe.

PRAYER:

"Jesus, I come to You today and ask that You help me to obey where I believe. I hear Your voice and thank You for the promises in Your Word to me. Help me take steps of faith and walk in Your victory. I receive Your grace that empowers me to obey. Thank You that my obedience does not cause You to love me more since You already love me perfectly, but I know that my obedience brings wonderful freedom in every area of my life and glorifies You. Amen."

DECLARATION:

"I am a doer of the Word, not just a hearer!" (James 1:22)

ACTION:

Where have you grown in your faith in God's Word and promises the last few weeks? How can you show your faith? Helping another? Encouraging someone? Praying for someone? Giving? Speaking the Word to yourself? Removing something from your life that discourages your faith? In other words, how can you start obeying God in a way that shows you truly believe what He says?

DAY 27: FREE TO OBEY

And having been set free from sin, you became slaves of righteousness. I speak in human terms because of the weakness of your flesh. For just as you presented your members as slaves of uncleanness, and of lawlessness leading to more lawlessness, so now present your members as slaves of righteousness for holiness (Romans 6:18-19).

When you know the truth that you have been set free, you will begin to live the obedient life that God has called you to live. Your faith in Jesus Christ has made you a new creation. You are a new person in Christ by grace through faith. When God transforms you on the inside, you are able to live a life of obedience and victory on the outside. You are a good tree in Christ, and since you are now a good tree, good fruit will abound in your words and actions (Matthew 7:17-20).

One of the greatest tragedies experienced by many people who have become born again through accepting Jesus Christ, is that they can become complacent and sloppy in their obedience to God. An attitude that says, "I'm saved by grace, not by works, so God understands when I fail and disobey God." God certainly understands, but He does not excuse our disobedience. God is grieved when we have a careless attitude toward obedience because He knows that sin and disobedience will always have hurtful consequences to ourselves and others. In fact, God hates sin because sin causes bondage and slavery. Obedience brings great blessings, but disobedience causes the trap and pain that you are seeking to come out from. Disobedience brings bondage; obedience brings about freedom.

The lie from the devil is that you are not able to stand in obedience and that you will always struggle. And since your struggle will always bring about disobedience and a careless attitude toward following God, you will always be stuck, trapped, and in a spiritual prison. Again, *this is a lie!*

In Romans chapter 6, the apostle Paul told the church in Rome that because they put their faith in Jesus, they no longer had to live under the enslavement of sin. The same goes for you. The sin that once held you captive was crucified and was buried with Jesus because He bore all sin on the cross.

Romans 6:7 says that the penalty and power of sin is dead; you have been set free (past tense). Romans 6:18 says, "And having been set free from sin, you became slaves of righteousness." You are free to obey God! You have the authority and ability to follow Jesus with all of your heart and to live in the righteousness of Christ. You are already righteous in Christ, so you can now live out of who you are!

> Your freedom is connected to your obedience, and your obedience is directly related to you knowing and living out the truth that you have already been set free.

The lie says that you are not free, but the truth says you are. The lie says that you are still a slave to sin and disobedience, but the truth says that you are *now* free to obey God with that same submission to His authority. You once submitted to sin, you've chosen to now submit to God. The fruit that comes from your life is now holiness, because you *have been* set free (Romans 6:22). The Holy Spirit passionately proclaims to you to consider your old self dead to sin, but alive in Christ (Romans 6:11). God says that you have the right to reject disobedience because it is no longer part of your new nature. Christ is in you; do not allow sin to reign in you because Jesus now reigns in you (Romans 6:12). Your freedom is connected to your obedience, and your obedience is directly related to you knowing and living out the truth that you have already been set free.

Reject the lie that you are not free. Accept the truth that you are free because Jesus is in you (Galatians 2:20). Now walk in that freedom. You are free to obey, and as you obey, you will continue to be free!

APPLICATION

WORSHIP:

Sing praises to the Lord for already setting you free. Focus on God's greatness and love. Thank Him over and over for providing the way of freedom.

PRAYER:

"Jesus, I want to obey You more. Thank You for making me free on the inside so I can obey You on the outside. Forgive me for the times that my attitude becomes careless to your holiness and I slack in obeying Your voice. I confess that there is nothing greater and nothing I desire more than to follow You wholly. I praise Your wonderful name for being faithful to me and crushing the enemy by setting me free. Amen!"

DECLARATION:

"I have been set free. Sin has no power over me. I am under grace." (Romans 6:14,18).

ACTION:

All day today, consider yourself free. Continue to read Romans 6:18 over and over. Do not stop until you truly believe this truth. God is not a liar. You are truly free because of Jesus. Talk and walk this way. This is who you really are!

DAY 28: FULLY SURRENDERED

I beseech you therefore, brethren, by the mercies of God, that you present your bodies a living sacrifice, holy, acceptable to God, which is your reasonable service. And do not be conformed to this world, but be transformed by the renewing of your mind, that you may prove what is that good and acceptable and perfect will of God (Romans 12:1-2).

Therefore we also, since we are surrounded by so great a cloud of witnesses, let us lay aside every weight, and the sin which so easily ensnares *us,* and let us run with endurance the race that is set before us, looking unto Jesus, the author and finisher of *our* faith, who for the joy that was set before Him endured the cross, despising the shame, and has sat down at the right hand of the throne of God (Hebrews 12:1-2).

True freedom comes to you through surrender. Obeying God is not done in the Christian life through your own efforts, sufficiency, strength, striving, or self-will. In fact, many even walk away from Christ because they become discouraged when it seems that there is no change, even when they try hard. The truth is that Jesus never calls us to obey Him without fully depending on Him first. Freedom to obey God does not come through our striving, but through offering ourselves to Him.

In the natural, *surrender* is a word that means defeat. When you read of the wars throughout mankind, the military that would surrender were the ones who would have lost. God's kingdom is much different. When you come to God and surrender, or give up your rights and place them in God's hands, you will always find victory and freedom.

> When you come to God and surrender, or give up your rights and place them in God's hands, you will always find victory and freedom.

Earlier we talked about the power of being transformed through renewing the mind with the Word of God (Romans 12:2). What is crucial to understand is that the verse preceding our transformation speaks of offering ourselves fully to God. It says that because we have been saved and set free by God's mercy, we are to offer ourselves, or surrender our lives fully, to God. When we choose to do this, it is holy and acceptable to God. In other words, our surrender to God is the beginning of our obedience to Him (Romans 12:1).

We can't obey God on our own. This should be evident and obvious as Jesus came to us because we needed to be saved. If we can't save ourselves due to sin, then we certainly can't obey God apart from Him either. I love how the author of Hebrews calls us to surrender fully to Jesus. Hebrews 12:1 says, "Let us lay aside every weight, and the sin that so easily ensnares us, and let us run with endurance the race that is set before us." Our freedom is directly related to our surrender. It says here to lay aside the weights that are heavily keeping us bound and the sin that trips us up and keeps us from living free. The call is not to try to work things out and try harder. God is calling you to surrender. Come the way you are, broken and hurt. Bring your failures and struggles and set them down in the presence of God. When you do surrender and tell God that you can't on your own, and you give God your bondage and inability to obey Him by yourself, God will begin to free you. This passage says that you will begin to run the race forward with endurance. The freedom that Jesus gives to you when you fully surrender to Him will make you feel light; you can breathe in the strength of the Spirit of God, and you can keep running forward in victory.

Not long after I received Jesus Christ, I began to sense God calling me to ministry, particularly to preach and teach the Word of God and to declare the good news. As I shared in a previous chapter, I was terrified of public speaking. So naturally, I said no. I was in a state of resisting God's call on my life out of fear. I was midway through high school, so it was important to start figuring out what I was going to do in my life as I prepared for college. There were so many career ideas that I thought of, but in the back of my mind I knew what I needed to do. As I thought through every career, even though it would have brought monetary success and prosperity, it was as if the Lord gave me a vision of my life working in these careers, and at the end of it, I was empty and miserable. Naturally, it didn't make sense, but in the kingdom of God, it made complete sense.

The pressure was on; I had no peace as I continued to wrestle with God and resist what He was calling me to. Then the day came; I knelt at my bedside in my room and fully surrendered to God. I wept like a baby and told Him that I would do what He wanted me to do and go wherever He wanted me to go. Was I nervous? Yes. Did I know what to do or have questions on how this would happen? No, and absolutely! But as I said, "Here I am," without fighting or quarreling with God and giving all of my rights to Him, a weight came off of me. I tell you, peace flooded my heart and I felt energized, passionate, and hungry to grow and obey God! I knew what God called me to, I surrendered to it, and by His grace I followed Him.

You do not need to live in frustration anymore. You need not get discouraged or overwhelmed with your struggle anymore. Jesus has won the victory. All He asks you to do is surrender. Perhaps there are areas of your life that you stubbornly hold onto, but it is the root of your defeat. Let it go. Don't strive; it gets you nowhere. Just offer yourself to Him and lay all that is not of Him before His throne. Jesus will not condemn you or push you away. He will embrace you, hold you, and lift you up as you surrender fully to Him. Your freedom and transformation will flourish as you surrender to God each moment.

APPLICATION

WORSHIP:

Surrender is worship because obeying God starts with surrender. In your quiet time with God, kneel before Him, raise your hands up to Him as an outward sign of what is in your heart. Tell Him that you surrender. You may weep before Him as you lay down your weights and sins. That is quite alright. Freedom is in surrender.

PRAYER:

"Jesus, I surrender to You. Take my struggle, my bondage, my failures, sins, weights, and mistakes. I look to You. All that I have and all that I am is Yours. You redeemed me from sin and death, so I give my life to You as an offering of thanksgiving and obedience. Thank You that I don't have to do this on my own, but as I surrender to You, I find freedom and the supernatural ability to follow You. I love You, Jesus. Amen."

DECLARATION:

"Because of God's grace and mercy in my life, I surrender fully to God." (Romans 12:1)

ACTION:

What are the weights that you can lay down before Jesus? Fear, anxiety, depression, discouragement, insecurity, or hurts? What are the sins that easily entangle you that you can lay down in God's loving presence? Jealousy, greed, lust, unforgiveness, hatred, or lying? As God's precious child, you do not need to carry this anymore. It's not your battle. Offer yourself to God, and as you do, lay these down once and for all. You will begin to feel the oppression that has pushed you down begin to leave and you will feel joy like never before in the presence of God.

DAY 29: PRACTICAL OBEDIENCE

Not lagging in diligence, fervent in spirit, serving the Lord (Romans 12:11).

For this reason we also, since the day we heard it, do not cease to pray for you, and to ask that you may be filled with the knowledge of His will in all wisdom and spiritual understanding; that you may walk worthy of the Lord, fully pleasing Him, being fruitful in every good work and increasing in the knowledge of God (Colossians 1:9-10).

When it comes to walking in freedom, God gives what is wise and practical. He speaks to us through His Word and the Holy Spirit, and says to gain knowledge, instruction, and wisdom from Him, and then He tells us to do it (Proverbs 2:1-7). *Applying* the truth is what sets you free.

Below are just a few practical applications that need to be lived out which will protect you from the snares of the devil and keep you on a path of freedom.

First of all, your freedom is tied to your relationships. You become who you hang out with. If you hang out with the wise, you will become wise (Proverbs 13:20). If you have close relationships that are against God and His Word, your character will become contaminated (1 Corinthians 15:33). God desires for you to get close to those who are close to Him. Find a strong Christian who has become free and is always growing in their relationship with God. You will find that you will become more like that person as they follow Jesus with all of their heart, mind, and strength.

This leads me to this truth: you will never grow in freedom unless you are actively involved and committed to a healthy, local church. The church is not man's idea; the church was started by Jesus. The church of Jesus Christ isn't a building; it is made up of every person who has been born again. The church is a community of believers who meet on a regular basis under godly authority, who feed on the preaching and teaching of the Word of God for the purpose of spiritual nourishment and growth (Ephesians 4:11-16). You will never grow or find the freedom that Jesus has called you to experience unless you are part of the local church. That is where you will continually grow in freedom by being fed the Word of God, encouraged through godly relationships, and held accountable to continue living free. It's where you can experience the presence of God in the company of other believers. God's heart and passion insist that you continue and serve in His church (Hebrews 10:25).

> God gives what is wise and practical. He speaks to us through His Word and the Holy Spirit, and says to gain knowledge, instruction, and wisdom from Him, and then He tells us to do it

Removing whatever obstacle that causes you to sin is paramount to experiencing freedom in Christ. Both gospels of Matthew and Mark state the importance of this principle. You really can't get more practical than this. The two gospels say that if your eye, foot, or hand causes you to sin, cut it off; it is better to live without something in the physical world than to lose spiritually. It is interesting that in Matthew's context, Jesus said to remove any hindrance that causes sin, which brings about bondage when it comes to lust (Matthew 5:27-30). Now Jesus is not saying to literally cut off your hand, eye, or foot. He is saying to remove anything in your life that causes you to remain stuck, trapped, and in bondage. Is there something you watch that you can get rid of? Is there a friend who is not a good influence on you who you need to distance yourself from? Is there a place you need to stop going to in order to keep you from falling? Jesus is being so practical. He is saying that if you make a decision to cut something out of your life and close the door to that which keeps you bound, then your freedom will become even easier because you will not have to fight the temptation every moment now that the "hand, eye, and foot" have been removed.

Be wise and be diligent to obey God. He has set up practical instructions throughout His Word for your benefit and blessing. Hear God, apply what He says, and you will be free!

APPLICATION

WORSHIP:

Sing praises to your Lord with diligent and relentless desire. Today is the day that the Lord has made. Rejoice in the Lord.

PRAYER:

"Lord, thank You for giving me practical steps and wisdom to protect my freedom in You. Give me the strength to make necessary decisions to grow in You and fully walk in Your ways. Be glorified as I walk in obedience. In Jesus' name. Amen."

DECLARATION:

"I walk worthy of the Lord, fully pleasing Him, and am fruitful in every good work" (Colossians 1:10).

ACTION:

Do you have great relationships with people who are close to God and are committed to following Jesus? If not, start walking this way. Are you actively a part of a healthy local church? If not, start looking for one. God will lead you to where you will be fed from God's Word and become free in Christ. Is there anything in your life that you need to cut off and remove that hinders your freedom? If so, start cutting it off. Nothing is worth more than your freedom.

DAY 30: ABIDING IN JESUS

I am the true vine, and My Father is the vinedresser. Every branch in Me that does not bear fruit He takes away; and every branch that bears fruit He prunes, that it may bear more fruit. You are already clean because of the word which I have spoken to you. Abide in Me, and I in you. As the branch cannot bear fruit of itself, unless it abides in the vine, neither can you, unless you abide in Me. I am the vine, you are the branches. He who abides in Me, and I in him, bears much fruit; for without Me you can do nothing. If anyone does not abide in Me, he is cast out as a branch and is withered; and they gather them and throw them into the fire, and they are burned. If you abide in Me, and My words abide in you, you will ask what you desire, and it shall be done for you. By this My Father is glorified, that you bear much fruit; so you will be My disciples (John 15:1-8).

God never intended for you to follow Him, obey Him, and listen to His voice in your own effort and strength. God is so good and gracious. He calls you to obey Him, which causes freedom and blessing to fill your life, but does not command you to obey and then leave it all up to you. You do not need to worry or fret, wondering and hoping that you will be free to obey God. Whatever God says in His Word for you to do, He gives you the power, grace, and provision to carry it out. God calls you to obey; God does it *in* you and *through* you! The Lord is committed to your freedom through obedience.

Jesus explains the relationship of Himself with you in a life-changing manner. He compares you and Himself to a vine and a branch. Picture a vineyard. Jesus is the vine. Within the vine are all the nutrients that are needed for the branch to be healthy. You are the branch. The branch receives all that it needs through the vine. The branch is able to produce much fruit because of the vine providing what the branch needs. In order for the branch to have fruit, it must abide. This word *abide* is the same word in the Greek that was shown on day 1 in this devotional. Again, the word is, *meno*, which means *to live, dwell, rest in, remain, continue.* Jesus said that as the branch rests, lives in, and depends on the vine, that *much* fruit will be the result. Literally, this word for *much* is the word *polys* which means *great in magnitude or quantity, large amount, a massive amount, or large amount!* The word for *fruit* here means *reward, profit, benefit.*

As you truly abide in Jesus, or continue to rest and depend on Him, you will experience such freedom when you obey Him because you will find that as you take steps of faith in obeying God, your sufficiency and ability will come from God. Jesus teaches a powerful truth here when it comes to following Him. Six times in this passage of just eight verses, Jesus says something that the branch receives as it abides in Him. The branch *bears* much fruit. Jesus *does not say* that the branch *produces* much fruit. Why didn't Jesus say that the branch needs to produce fruit? Because a branch can't produce fruit (John 15:4-5). The branch must abide and rest on the vine for the fruit to come forth. The vine produces the fruit for the branch, the branch depends and dwells upon the vine and receives from the vine. Resting, depending, and making your home in Jesus will cause you to bear and receive the reward and benefits that come from Jesus.

How does Jesus give you what is needed to bear fruit? What are the nutrients that Jesus says will energize you and empower you to bear fruit that will last as you obey God by being connected to Him? His presence and His words that are already in you produce the fruit because you rest, depend, and live in Jesus and His Word. Jesus said, "Abide in Me, and I in you...if you abide in Me, and My words abide in you" (John 15:4, 7).

If God intended for you to obey Him by striving, pushing, and figuring out how to be free on your own, then Jesus would have never said to abide in Him. Rather, Jesus said that you cannot do anything without Him (John 15:5). Just as a branch that is not connected to the vine will wither and not bear fruit, so you desperately need to depend fully on the vine, Jesus, to be filled with all that you need to obey and run this race in freedom.

> ## If God intended for you to obey Him by striving, pushing, and figuring out how to be free on your own, then Jesus would have never said to abide in Him.

Bearing much fruit, by resting on Jesus, will free you from independently living the life God called you to live, to receive all that you need for life and godliness through Him alone. Jesus produces fruit; you bear the fruit that Jesus produces. Living by this truth will enable you to obey God and live in freedom.

APPLICATION

WORSHIP:

Raise your hands as you sing to your Lord. Worship God by trading in your self-efforts for total dependence on the presence of God and His words that are in you. Worship and glorify Jesus by resting in Him. Sit in quiet expectation as the branch in God's presence. Allow Him to fill you as you abide in Him.

PRAYER:

"Jesus, I thank You for being the vine, the One whom I need to depend on, rest in, and dwell upon. You give me all that is needed to obey You, be free in You, and bear the fruit that You want me to bear. I confess that I can't do this without You, but I can do it with You. As I put my faith in Your Word and take steps to obey, I thank You that You produce all that I need. Thank You for positioning me for freedom, not by trying and failing on my own, but through leaning on You and allowing Your presence and Word to change me, free me, and enable me to walk in Your ways. I abide in You, in Jesus' name. Amen."

DECLARATION:

"I bear a large amount of fruit because I remain dependent on Jesus to produce the fruit in me and through me" (John 15:5).

ACTION:

What area of life are you wanting freedom in? How have you tried to be free in the past? What area do you find yourself falling and failing, where it has come to the point of great frustration and discouragement? Take inventory and ask yourself these questions:

1. Are you trying and working hard without depending fully on Jesus to give you what is needed to obey?

2. Have you believed the lie that you can do it on your own?

3. Do you believe the lie that God is disappointed with you and that He is like a taskmaster, telling you to get it straight and obey His law?

4. Have you spent time with Jesus, intentionally telling Him that you will rest and depend on Him?

5. Are you depending on your self-effort and self-sufficiency to obey the law of God, or are you receiving the amazing grace of God that calls you to Himself, resting as a branch does on the vine, and letting God produce the fruit in you? Freedom comes to the one fully dependent on Jesus. Dependence on Him for obedience glorifies God and brings pleasure to Him as He sees His children bear much fruit.

PART VII : PRAY

Pursue God

DAY 31: A YES GOD

Ask, and it will be given to you; seek, and you will find; knock, and it will be opened to you. For everyone who asks receives, and he who seeks finds, and to him who knocks it will be opened. Or what man is there among you who, if his son asks for bread, will give him a stone? Or if he asks for a fish, will he give him a serpent? If you then, being evil, know how to give good gifts to your children, how much more will your Father who is in heaven give good things to those who ask Him! Therefore, whatever you want men to do to you, do also to them, for this is the Law and the Prophets (Matthew 7:7-12).

One of the most fundamental practices that breaks the chains of bondage into pieces is praying to the Lord. Prayer is simply authentic communication with God.

Communication involves both talking and listening; both are necessary ingredients to prayer. The truth is, you cannot know Jesus more unless you have communication with Him on a daily basis. Prayer is not a religious, boring duty that Christians are just called to partake in. Prayer is an awesome privilege, an exciting adventure, where you bear your heart to God, ask and petition Him for the miraculous, draw close to hearing His heart and voice, and grow in knowing and believing Him. Prayer offered to God with a heart that is fully surrendered and full of faith is powerful and effective in your life and in the lives of others you are interceding for (James 5:15-16).

God is a yes God! God is willing and able to answer your prayer, especially when it comes to your freedom. He is so concerned and committed to seeing every single bondage that traps you, whether it is a lie that condemns you, a way of thinking that keeps you down, or an addiction that you can't seem to fully defeat, be fully annihilated. Many are deceived into thinking that they need to bribe, beg, or manipulate their case before God. They believe the lie that God will usually answer, *no,* to their prayers. While God does answer no at times, especially if our motive is wrong or the prayers are not aligned with His Word and nature, God is waiting for you to come to Him, and ask of Him, so that He can say yes and move in a life-changing, miraculous way.

God is willing and able to answer your prayer, especially when it comes to your freedom.

Jesus encourages you to ask Him, seek Him, and knock on the door as you pray. His promise for everyone who asks is that they *will* receive. The individual who seeks, *will* find. For the one who knocks, the door *will* be opened. Jesus did not provide for any ounce of doubt as you pray. He said the answer from God is that He WILL. God is a yes God when you pray. Jesus further provides assurance by revealing the nature of our heavenly Father. Jesus goes on to say that if a son asks for bread, would an earthly father give him a stone? If a son asks his dad for fish, would the earthly father give him a serpent? The answer is, "of course not!" Jesus said, if an earthly father, who loves his son, would never do such a thing even as a fallen, imperfect dad, then why in the world would we think our perfect, loving Father in heaven would do such a thing to His precious sons and daughters? Yet, many do not pray because they have a false picture of the willingness and desire of God to answer prayer. The quality and quantity of your prayer life is directly related to how you view God, whether by truth or a lie.

We have just read about the power of abiding in Jesus and Jesus abiding in us. When Jesus abides in us, His words abide in us. One of the promises of abiding is that we are so full of knowing Jesus, that we will desire what God desires. When we ask what we desire, because we are one with Jesus, it shall be done for us. God is a yes God! You pray and He is willing to do it! Jesus said, "If you ask anything in My name, I *will* do it" (John 14:14). He says in Mark 11:24, "whatever things you ask when you pray, believe that you receive them, and you *will* have them."

Jesus leaves no room for doubt. You pray; God will answer. He didn't say He might, or He will think about it, or will see if you deserve it. God said pray, and He will! How encouraging and motivating to know that God says yes!

APPLICATION

WORSHIP:

It is not hard to worship and adore God knowing that He is a yes God. The Lord loves to answer your prayers and touch your heart. Sing and thank your God with excitement and expectation that He is answering your prayer.

PRAYER:

"Lord Jesus, I thank You that each prayer I have prayed during these days, You have answered, and are answering. I know that I am receiving, finding, and the door is opening, because You want to answer me. I pray for full freedom in every area of my life. I praise You for the answer and that You are my God who says yes. Remove every lie that says that You are reluctant to answer me; I take a hold of Your willingness to answer me. In Jesus' name. Amen!"

DECLARATION:

"I am a child of the Father and I receive good gifts and good answers from Him because I ask Him through prayer."

ACTION:

Remove any lie that God does not care and that God will never say yes. When it comes to your victory and freedom, God will *always* say yes. His will is to free you fully. Come to Jesus and pray. Ask, seek, and knock. Watch what God does because He is for you and says yes!

DAY 32: IN THE NAME OF JESUS

Most assuredly, I say to you, he who believes in Me, the works that I do he will do also; and greater works than these he will do, because I go to My Father. And whatever you ask in My name, that I will do, that the Father may be glorified in the Son. If you ask anything in My name, I will do it (John 14:12-14).

One of the greatest gifts that Jesus has given to every believer who prays and demands the kingdom of darkness to get out and to release you and others, is the gift of His name. One of the amazing truths that Jesus taught His last week on earth and before going to the cross is the power of His name, and the privilege for every single believer to use His name for freedom and victory.

Acts 10:38 says that the Holy Spirit anointed Jesus with power, and He did good, healing all who were oppressed by the devil. Jesus taught the truth that set people free, He healed disease, He cast out demons from people, He calmed the storm, and did so much when He was on this earth in a physical body. Before He went to die on a cross, rise again, and ascend to heaven, Jesus told his disciples that all who put their faith in Him for salvation will do what He did. In fact, every believer would be doing greater works (John 14:12). Jesus said that the greater works of teaching, preaching, healing, and doing the miraculous in people's lives would be through His name. *The promise of Jesus is that when you ask of God, and demand the devil, in the name of Jesus, it will be done.*

Those who were listening to what Jesus was saying about using His name understood well. The political culture during this time included kings as rulers of the land. Different empires and kingdoms were led by the king, and whatever the king commanded or decreed, it was the law. It could not be altered or changed. We see this in the book of Esther. Haman was the chief minister under King Ahasuerus. The king commanded all of his servants to bow and pay homage to Haman. Haman hated the fact that Mordecai, a Jew who served in the palace, would not bow. So Haman went to the king and fabricated the story of how terrible the Jews were in the land. He asked the king to write a decree to destroy all the Jews on a certain day in the land of Persia. The decree was written in the king's name, and the couriers of that day went out in all the land, declaring the law in the king's name (Esther 3:12-15). Thankfully, the evil plot was exposed, and King Ahasuerus told Queen Esther to write another law to save the Jews. He told her to write the decree in his name and to seal it with the king's signet ring. Esther 8:8 says, "For whatever is written in the king's name and sealed with the king's signet ring no one can revoke." The decree was then proclaimed in the name of the king, and the Jews were saved. They celebrated with a feast, and with joy and gladness.

Jesus is calling you to take your authority that has been given to you from Him and be a courier.

Jesus is the King of kings (Revelation 19:16). There is no one greater than Jesus. All power and authority are in Him. Philippians 2:9-11 says that every knee will one day bow before Him; whether the angels in heaven, every human being that has ever lived on earth, every demonic force, or the devil himself, for there is no name comparable to Jesus.

King Jesus has written a decree; His Word, that cannot be revoked. Jesus is calling you to take your authority that has been given to you from Him and be a courier. Proclaim the decree of freedom to yourself and to others, in the name of Jesus! You do not come in your own authority or with your own clever ideas to become free. When you pray to the Lord about what you need and the needs of others, you are agreeing with the eternal decree and promises of God! When you command the power of darkness to leave, command the body to be healed, tell fear and anxiety to take a hike, and destroy the works of the devil, you do so in the name of Jesus! Every other authority that is against you must submit and bow its knee, because you come and declare the truth, in the name of the King of kings, Jesus! Use the name of Jesus, and greater works will be done! Ask God anything that God says in His Word, and it will come to pass! As you pray in the name of Jesus, you will do good and heal all who are oppressed of the devil, for Jesus is with you.

APPLICATION

WORSHIP:

Worship your King. Jesus is highly exalted, and nothing can come against His words or power! Sing to Him, "Holy, holy, holy is the Lord God Almighty!" Celebrate the name of Jesus with joy and gladness.

PRAYER:

"Jesus, thank You for giving me authority in Your name. I realize that when I pray in Your name, I have access to You, authority in Your name, and I agree with the eternal decree of Your Word. I pray for freedom and I renounce and rebuke the work of Satan over _____ in my life and in the life of _____. I believe that I receive, in the name of Jesus. Amen!"

DECLARATION:

"God will do whatever I ask, in the name of Jesus, because the decree has been written for my freedom" (John 14:13-14).

ACTION:

The days of praying to God in a timid fashion are over. King Jesus said to use His powerful name, and what He did on earth you will do on earth, because the name of Jesus represents who is doing the work. What needs do you have? Begin to ask God, intentionally and with careful thought, in the name of Jesus. Understand what you are saying when you pray in the name of Jesus. How is the devil attacking you, your family, your church, or a friend that is in need? Renounce the works of Satan in the name of Jesus.

DAY 33: APPROACHABLE

Then He spoke a parable to them, that men always ought to pray and not lose heart, saying: "There was in a certain city a judge who did not fear God nor regard man. Now there was a widow in that city; and she came to him, saying, 'Get justice for me from my adversary.' And he would not for a while; but afterward he said within himself, 'Though I do not fear God nor regard man, yet because this widow troubles me I will avenge her, lest by her continual coming she weary me.' " Then the Lord said, "Hear what the unjust judge said. And shall God not avenge His own elect who cry out day and night to Him, though He bears long with them? I tell you that He will avenge them speedily. Nevertheless, when the Son of Man comes, will He really find faith on the earth?" (Luke 18:1-8).

Prayer is a key that will unlock the door to your freedom. The devil knows this and will keep you from spending time in prayer with God. He will deceive you into thinking that prayer is a dry, boring, mundane, religious act that will only feel like you are talking to a brick wall. That is a lie, and is the devil's way of keeping you off your knees and from talking and listening to God. The other lie that many fall for is that God is not interested in your problems or your requests that come from the heart. Since you have the wrong picture of God and feel unworthy to approach God, you fail to pray. Both are strategic schemes that the devil uses, and they work well against the uninformed believer. It is important for you to know that prayer frees you, but you must be free to pray so you can pray in faith and power.

Jesus puts this false picture of God to rest in a parable, or a story that teaches a spiritual truth. He said that there was a widow who was in great need because an adversary was causing injustice in her life. Having an adversary was just the icing on the cake for her life because back in this time and culture, a widow was not in a favorable standing socially or economically. She needed help from the law, so she went to a judge. The problem was that the judge did not fear God or care for human beings. He would hear the widow's concern, but did not budge. He didn't care that the widow was in trouble, and did not care what the adversary was doing to her, even if it was illegal. But eventually the judge surprisingly answered the widow and helped her. It wasn't because he cared, but because he was bothered by her continually coming to him. The widow troubled him and made him weary by her consistent request.

> God is calling you to come to Him anytime and with boldness. You have a right to come to His throne room as His son or daughter. You have been invited.

Jesus was not using this parable as a *comparison* of what we are like and how God responds to us when we make requests. Jesus used this parable as a *contrast* of who we are and how God responds. After all, Jesus used this parable to encourage us to continue in prayer and to be encouraged, not discouraged. We are not like the widow, helpless and forgotten. We are sons and daughters of God. We are not beggars, trying to get God's attention for Him to answer. We are not being a pest in the ears of God, trying to make Him so sick of us that He finally answers. We do not bribe or manipulate Him. As sons and daughters, we have access to Him because we are in a relationship with Him. God is not an unjust judge. As sons and daughters, we come to a loving, heavenly Father. He longs to speak to us, encourage us, answer our prayers, help us, do the miraculous, and set us free. Our Father invites us to commune with Him and talk with Him. He wants to hear from our hearts: our struggles, our fears, our bondage, our joy, our laughter, and our victories. Father and son, Father and daughter. He answers our prayers so that our joy is full (John 16:24).

God is calling you to come to Him anytime and with boldness. You have a right to come to His throne room as His son or daughter. You have been invited. When you come to God in prayer, you come to the presence of God, and to His throne of grace. When you come into the presence of God and pray, you will always "obtain mercy and find grace to help in time of need" (Hebrews 4:16). Mercy is God not giving you what you deserve, and grace is God giving to you what you do not deserve.

God wants you free from this day forward. Prayer will free you, but you need to be free to pray. Knowing the truth that God is approachable and waiting for you to experience His mercy and grace whenever you come to Him will empower you and encourage you to continue in prayer. Throw off the lies that God is not interested, that prayer is boring, and you will not find freedom as you pray. Come boldly to the throne of grace. Declare in faith and with authority that you are free and that the chains which have held you captive have been destroyed!

APPLICATION

WORSHIP:

As you worship Jesus, know that you enter boldly into His throne room. You are invited; you have direct access into God's presence through the blood of Jesus. The veil has been torn; come boldly and obtain mercy and grace. Praise the Lord for His invitation and worship Him for being a great God.

PRAYER:

"Jesus, I come boldly to You. Thank You that as Your child, I can come to You at any time and You never cast me out. I praise Your name for loving me and receiving me. Remove once and for all the lie that You don't care and that You won't answer me. I receive Your answer to my freedom; I receive freedom in Your presence. I pray for (insert what you are believing for here) and believe that I receive it. In Jesus' name. Amen."

DECLARATION:

"I boldly come to Jesus in prayer and receive the answer because of His mercy and grace" (Hebrews 4:16).

ACTION:

Begin to believe that God is ready to hear and answer you (Jeremiah 29:12). God will listen and answer you. God loves spending time with you and will do everything according to His promise and His power in your life. Now pray. Come boldly, not as a beggar, but as a righteous, worthy, child of God. You have the right and privilege to pray; get alone with God and receive all that you need in His holy presence.

DAY 34: THE POWER OF TONGUES

When the Day of Pentecost had fully come, they were all with one accord in one place. And suddenly there came a sound from heaven, as of a rushing mighty wind, and it filled the whole house where they were sitting. Then there appeared to them divided tongues, as of fire, and *one* sat upon each of them. And they were all filled with the Holy Spirit and began to speak with other tongues, as the Spirit gave them utterance (Acts 2:1-4).

God's Word says, "Death and life are in the power of the tongue, and those who love it will eat its fruit" (Proverbs 18:21). How wonderful a gift that God has promised for every believer in Christ to receive the baptism, or immersion, in the Holy Spirit. This experience is a life-changing experience of the empowerment of the Holy Spirit to be a witness and to receive the language that God gives. Tongues, when used in prayer and praise, will bring destruction to the kingdom of darkness and life and freedom to you. Your tongue can bring that which is dead to life by allowing the Holy Spirit to give you utterance to pray from your spirit in the unknown language that comes out of your mouth called tongues.

When you are born again, the Holy Spirit immediately comes to live on the *inside* of you and is the guarantee of your salvation (Romans 8:11; Ephesians 1:13-14). When Jesus rose from the dead, He breathed on the disciples to receive the Holy Spirit (John 20:22). This was the beginning of the new birth experience. Just as God breathed life into man to give him life at creation, so Jesus breathed life into His disciples for the new birth. From that day forward, everyone who believed and received Jesus for the forgiveness of sins received the indwelling presence of the Holy Spirit, which is now in you as a fountain of water springing up into everlasting life (John 4:14). You never have to thirst again because all of the Holy Spirit is in you!

Jesus said that there was another experience for every believer, which is called the baptism in the Holy Spirit. Jesus commanded His disciples to wait for the promise, or baptism in the Holy Spirit. Jesus said, "You shall be baptized with the Holy Spirit" (Acts 1:5). This is when the Holy Spirit, who is already in you, comes *upon you* for power to be witnesses. At salvation, the Holy Spirit comes in you, but during the baptism in the Holy Spirit, you are immersed in Him and He flows out of you. Jesus explained this in John 7:38-39 by saying, "Out of his heart will flow rivers of living water. But this He spoke concerning the Spirit, whom those believing in Him would receive." Jesus said that one of the signs that follow those who believe in Him was that "They will speak with new tongues" (Mark 16:17).

In Acts 2, the disciples obeyed Jesus, and as they were assembled, they were all filled with the Holy Spirit, and they all began to speak in tongues. This was the Promise of the Holy Spirit that Jesus said would be the baptism in the Holy Spirit (Acts 1:4-5), which happened to every believer in the upper room on the day of Pentecost. The evidence was that they spoke in tongues as the Holy Spirit gave them the words that came out of their mouths.

The apostle Paul said that praying in tongues is praying from your spirit, not your mind (1 Corinthians 14:14). The Holy Spirit, who made your spirit come alive when you were born again, enables you to pray in tongues when you are baptized in the Holy Spirit, or filled with the Holy Spirit. When the Holy Spirit gives you the tongue, or language to pray, the Holy Spirit prays the perfect will of God and intercedes through your speaking in tongues. Paul said that praying in tongues is praying with your spirit through the Holy Spirit. He said to pray *in the Spirit* and to pray with understanding, or pray in tongues (that which your mind does not comprehend) as well as pray to God in your own language (1 Corinthians 14:15). Both are beneficial; one is not more important than the other, but to miss out on praying in tongues is to miss out on the will of God and amazing blessings!

Praying in tongues is powerful and thwarts the devil and the kingdom of darkness. The devil hates when you pray in tongues because it is the Holy Spirit praying through you. You may not understand with your mind what you are praying, but you trust in the words that the Holy Spirit is praying through you, both for yourself and others.

After exhorting the believers in Ephesus to put on the armor of God to stand against the devil, Paul ends by saying, "Praying always with all prayer and supplication in the Spirit" (Ephesians 6:18). Praying in the Spirit is praying in tongues, as Paul explained in 1 Corinthians 14:15. It is necessary and powerful to defeat the devil and to bring freedom to your life.

> When you pray and speak the wonderful words and works of God through praying in tongues, freedom will be experienced.

Praying in tongues not only pushes the enemy back, but it edifies you (1 Corinthians 14:4). The apostle Paul spoke in tongues on a regular basis (1 Corinthians 14:18). He needed the Holy Spirit to build Him up and to pray on His behalf.

How interesting it is that God chose what comes out of your mouth—tongues—to be a weapon that defeats those things that come against you to defeat you. You can't pray in tongues without moving your mouth and speaking. When you pray and speak the wonderful words and works of God through praying in tongues, freedom will be experienced. The devil will flee, and God will be glorified. Learn the power of praying in tongues. Life and freedom will be the result! The promise is for you and your children (Acts 2:38-39).

APPLICATION

WORSHIP:

If you have been baptized with the Holy Spirit and you speak with tongues, worship God by singing in the Spirit, as the apostle Paul's custom was.

PRAYER:

"Jesus, I thank You for Your promise of baptizing me in the Holy Spirit. I worship You and pray in the Holy Spirit by praying in tongues. Thank You, Holy Spirit, for giving me the utterance and ability to speak the language that You give to me which prays and speaks the perfect will of God. I know that as I pray in tongues, You intercede for me and for others. I accept all that You give to me and thank You for the blessing and gift of praying in tongues. Free me and edify me as I pray in tongues; free others and destroy the works of darkness, in Jesus' name. Amen."

DECLARATION:

"I pray boldly in the Holy Spirit and thank Jesus for the power of praying in tongues."

ACTION:

John the Baptist foretold that Jesus would come and said, "I indeed baptize you with water…He will baptize you with the Holy Spirit and fire" (Luke 3:16). Jesus referred to what John the Baptist said in Acts 1:5 by saying, "For John truly baptized with water, but you shall be baptized with the Holy Spirit." When the Holy Spirit baptized and filled the disciples in Acts 2, they spoke with tongues.

Have you been baptized in the Holy Spirit? If you haven't, turn to the *Appendix* in the back of the book, and pray to receive the infilling of the Holy Spirit with the evidence of speaking in tongues. You don't want to miss what God has for you. Your freedom is connected to the baptism in the Holy Spirit and praying in tongues. If you have been baptized and speak in tongues but it is not a priority, renew that priority again. Pray in tongues throughout the day today. Watch what God will do in you and through you!

DAY 35: BE STILL

Be still, and know that I *am* God; I will be exalted among
the nations, I will be exalted in the earth! (Psalm 46:10)

Being still in God's presence must be learned and cultivated, especially in this busy life. Prayer is communication with God, which includes listening to God. God wants you to pray in faith to experience freedom and answered prayer, but many forfeit freedom because they fail to sit still and allow God to fight the battle. When David made war with Goliath, the freedom of Israel was at stake. He knew that the giant would be defeated because he said that "the battle is the Lord's" (1 Samuel 17:47). When the enemy armies came against King Jehoshophat, he sought the Lord in prayer. God answered and said, "You will not need to fight in this battle. Position yourselves, stand still and see the salvation of the Lord, who is with you" (2 Chronicles 20:17). Listening to God and hearing His direction for your life will be hard if you will not be still.

There are many times when the writers of the Gospels showed how Jesus often withdrew to pray (Luke 5:16; 22:41; Matthew 14:23; Mark 6:46). There were many who wanted to hear Jesus teach, and they needed His word and touch to heal them. His schedule was always busy, so He knew the importance of spending time with the Father alone. This is why the disciples asked Him to teach them how to pray (Luke 11:1). They saw what happened when Jesus prayed and wanted the same results. Jesus said, "When you pray, go into your room, and when you have shut your door, pray to your Father who is in the secret place; and your Father who sees in secret will reward you openly" (Matthew 6:6). Getting alone and getting away from all distractions of life is crucial to receive all that God has for you. When you meet God and seek Him in the quiet place, He will speak. You will know and hear God in the stillness.

Wonderful peace and confidence comes when you are *still* in God's presence. Isaiah 30:15 says, "In quietness and confidence shall be your strength." You will find such strength to overcome and live in freedom by being still in God's presence. Paul said that through prayer it is possible to be free from worry and anxiety. He says, "Be anxious for nothing, but in everything by prayer and supplication, with thanksgiving, let your requests be made known to God; and the peace of God, which surpasses all understanding, will guard your hearts and minds through Christ Jesus" (Philippians 4:6-7). You gain great strength, peace, and confidence when you sit in God's presence because you cease fighting, battling, and working things out in your own wisdom and power. Stress flees from you because you hand over all your baggage and the things that bind you to God. Choosing to be still and choosing to cease striving in God's presence will free you because where the Spirit of the Lord is there is liberty and freedom (2 Corinthians 3:17).

> You gain great strength, peace, and confidence when you sit in God's presence because you cease fighting, battling, and working things out in your own wisdom and power.

Be still and you will know God more. When you choose to be still with God, you know Him more because you seek His face. You hunger to know *Him* before what He can give. Your greatest reward is Jesus, not what miracle He performs first. God is committed to answer your prayers, petitions, and intercessions. The hand of the Lord is mighty to save and set free, but before your freedom is manifested by His mighty hand, God wants you to know Him by seeking His face. True freedom in prayer is not just found by believing and receiving from the hand of God, but by sitting still and receiving God Himself. God is not a genie where you hand Him a wish list and check it off as it is answered. He wants a relationship with you above all else. As you hunger to know Him, listen to Him, fellowship with Him, and share your heart with Him, freedom will abound in your life. God told David to seek His face. David answers by saying, "My heart said to You, "Your face, Lord, I will seek"" (Psalm 27:8).

APPLICATION

WORSHIP:

As you come into the presence of God to worship today, be still at first. Shut off everything around you. Get alone. Sit and receive God's great love and love Him by sitting quietly. Focus fully on Him. Worship Him in the stillness.

PRAYER:

"Lord, how I often define prayer by talking only. Help me to learn to be quiet and still to listen to You. You have much to communicate to me, but I know that it is not always instruction. I am so thankful that You desire to just love me, hold me, comfort me, fellowship with me, and laugh with me. Thank You that You free me in Your wonderfully safe and loving presence. I hunger to come to You daily and be still and let You be God. Amen."

DECLARATION:

"I am set free in God's presence. I am still before my God so that I know the great I AM." (Psalm 46:10; 2 Corinthians 3:16)

ACTION:

Communication is the balance of talking and listening. Usually we think that in order for God to answer our prayers for freedom we need to talk and remind Him of what we have already petitioned for. One of the greatest ways to receive from God is to be still before Him, trusting that He is God and has all things under control. Many times when you sit before God, you are reminded by Him of what He has promised and what He is already fighting for. How is your communication with God? Is it one-sided with talking only? He loves hearing your heart, but He loves when you rest in Him and just listen to Him. Today, practice listening. Be still. Don't miss out on what God has for you because you are too stressed and worried giving all your petitions. Watch how free you become by being still at the feet of Jesus.

PART VIII: PRAISE

REJOICE IN THE LORD

DAY 36: CHAOS IN THE ENEMY'S CAMP

Now when they began to sing and to praise, the Lord set
ambushes against the people of Ammon, Moab, and Mount
Seir, who had come against Judah; and they were defeated.
For the people of Ammon and Moab stood up against the
inhabitants of Mount Seir to utterly kill and destroy *them*.
And when they had made an end of the inhabitants of Seir,
they helped to destroy one another. So when Judah came to
a place overlooking the wilderness, they looked toward the
multitude; and there *were* their dead bodies, fallen on the
earth. No one had escaped (2 Chronicles 20:22-24).

Praise is the environment of freedom and liberty. Wherever authentic
praise is offered to God, those things that try to bind and keep you
imprisoned crash to the ground. The enemy of your heart, mind,
and body cannot stick around where praise is happening. Every demonic
force against you becomes confused, panic-stricken, and overcome as
their plans topple over in the presence of praise given to the Most High
God. If you want to live daily in freedom, you must become a person of
perpetual praise.

Why is praise so powerful and connected to your freedom? It is
because God inhabits—or is enthroned in—the praise of His people (see
Psalm 22:3). God is King and His kingdom has no end. He chooses to
manifest His presence and kingdom in the midst of people who praise,
adore, glorify, and worship Him. Praise is declaring the awesome majesty
and power of God. Praise is humble worship and adoration. Praise is
calling out to God with the understanding that He alone is worthy of all

the glory and is able to do above and beyond what is asked for. Praising God is having faith and thanksgiving in what God has done and declaring that He is faithful to do it again. Praise declares the victory and is the celebration of the war that has been won!

Wherever authentic praise is offered to God, those things that try to bind and keep you imprisoned crash to the ground.

There is an amazing story that unfolds in 2 Chronicles chapter 20 and I encourage you to read the whole chapter. A great multitude of enemies were coming, and when King Jehoshophat heard the news he initially reacted out of fear. When he feared, he did what he knew was the best response; he sought the Lord and proclaimed a fast throughout all of Judah. In his humble prayer, Jehoshophat said, "O our God, will You not judge them? For we have no power against this great multitude that is coming against us; nor do we know what to do, but our eyes are upon You" (2 Chronicles 20:12). The Spirit of the Lord came upon Jahaziel and instructed Jehoshophat and those listening not to be discouraged or fear because the battle was the Lord's. Jehoshophat responded to the word of the Lord with humility, bowed before His God, and worshipped the Lord.

The next morning, they went out to position themselves in battle against the enemy. King Jehoshophat did something that military intelligence would never recommend. He "Appointed those who should sing to the Lord, and who should praise the beauty of holiness, as they went out before the army and were saying: 'Praise the Lord, For His mercy endures forever'" (2 Chronicles 20:21). Those who praised the Lord led the army into battle, but the army did not have to fight this battle, for the battle was the Lord's. This passage continues to say that when they began to sing and praise, God's presence and rulership was manifested. How? The Lord Himself set ambushes against the enemy. The enemy destroyed themselves in the midst of chaos and confusion in the camp. God won the battle in the midst of the people's praise. Praise invites and adores God's presence, and wherever God is present, there is freedom and victory.

What is the enemy fighting you with? What is he threatening your freedom in Christ with? No matter what you are becoming free in and no matter what journey you have been on so far, begin to praise the Lord. Sing loud and with joyful thanksgiving. Declare His greatness and goodness, worship Him, and let your praises confuse, shock, and utterly destroy the enemy in your life. God is enthroned and dwells in your praises. His presence is no match for any enemy. Praise the Lord and be free!

APPLICATION

WORSHIP:

Sing praises to God. If you need to, start by finding a worship song that helps you connect with God. He loves your worship, and you will find that as you praise God, you will feel free. The reason is that your attention is on God who is with you, and where the Spirit is, there is freedom!

PRAYER:

"Lord, how I want to grow in my praise to You. I love You and praise Your holy name. You are so good and so kind. You have done so much in my life and through my life. I praise You and know You have provided for my freedom, won in Your presence. I realize that You are with me all the time, but You manifest Your presence in a special way as I praise You. I praise You and rejoice in battling the enemy that is against me. I trust You and love You as I praise. In Jesus' name. Amen."

DECLARATION:

"I will greatly praise the Lord with my mouth; Yes, I will praise Him among the multitude" (Psalm 109:30).

ACTION:

Do you praise God on a continual basis? Is there a song in your heart because you are filled with love and thanksgiving to God? Start praising, even now. Make it a point to sing to God. Perhaps you need to be free because you lack in your praise to God. Switch off the music you are used to and put on worship and praise. Watch what happens in your heart and in your mouth.

Understand two things when you praise the Lord:

1. You need to praise the Lord *before* your freedom comes. Many do not praise God because they are waiting for answered prayer or to overcome first. King Jehoshophat led with praise, and then the enemy was defeated.

2. Praising the Lord *results* in freedom. 2 Chronicles 20:30 says, "Then the realm of Jehoshophat was quiet, for his God gave him rest all around." There are great things in store for the one who praises God from the heart and out of the mouth.

DAY 37: THE CHAINS ARE FALLING

But at midnight Paul and Silas were praying and singing hymns to God, and the prisoners were listening to them. Suddenly there was a great earthquake, so that the foundations of the prison were shaken; and immediately all the doors were opened and everyone's chains were loosed (Acts 16:25-26).

In Acts 16:16-34 there is a story about how Paul and Silas had gone to prayer and were met by a certain slave girl who was possessed by a spirit of divination. This girl brought much profit to her master by fortunetelling. This demonic spirit continually harassed Paul and Silas wherever they went. Finally, Paul took authority and cast it out of her in the name of Jesus. The girl's masters were furious and seized them, dragged them to the city officials, and accused Paul and Silas of causing trouble in the city. The city magistrates commanded that they be beaten by rods and scourged, or whipped. After going through this torture, they were thrown into the inner prison and chained up.

This seemed to be an unfair situation. While on their way to a prayer meeting, Paul and Silas ministered the gospel and freed a girl from a demon spirit, and what was their reward? They were falsely accused, beaten, whipped, thrown into prison, and chained up. The situation they were in was certainly an excuse to complain, doubt God, wonder if they were following the will of God, and grounds to walk away from obeying God. Paul and Silas were trapped, in prison, and bound in chains. The pain that they felt in their bodies was unbearable. The prison they were thrown into was dark, damp, and rat-infested. The circumstances were not favorable and there was no way out—or so it seemed!

As Paul and Silas were chained up, in prison, and in severe pain, they began to do something that is out of the ordinary in such a situation. Though they were bound, they did something that was not natural and went against human logic. They began to pray and then praise the Lord! While they were experiencing the pain, the prison, and the shackles, they put on the praise. This decision did not make sense! Yet they praised the God who makes the possible happen in impossible situations.

Suddenly the earth shook, the prison was rocked at its foundation, all the prison doors burst open, and the chains were loosed. God set Paul and Silas free as they praised Him! In the middle of the circumstances holding Paul and Silas captive, they sang songs of praise loud and clear to the Lord. Their worship did not stop during their trial. The pain of being persecuted and bound did not stop their praise because they knew that God was still on the throne and nothing was able to keep Him from setting them free.

What's even more amazing is that God wasn't done. In fact, all of the prisoners were able to be freed from the chains that bound them. The prison guard was so terrified that he had failed at keeping the prisoners bound that he was about to kill himself. But before he could end his life, Paul called out to assure the guard that none of the prisoners had fled. This led to the guard's salvation; he and his whole family! That night the guard's whole family was baptized, which led to even more rejoicing and praise for the Lord because a lost sinner had found life in Jesus.

God is worthy of praise, even when the chains still seem to be fastened to you. God never changes and His presence is enthroned in your praise. The Lord will change your circumstances and free you suddenly as you praise him from your lips and worship Him from your heart. No prison or bondage has the power to withstand the hand of the Lord. As you become a person of praise, God will not only free you, but will change the lives of people all around you.

The kingdom of darkness has no hold on the person who makes praising God the practice of their life. Give praise to God for who He is, for what He has done, for what He is doing for you now, and for what great power He will show to destroy every chain that tries to bind you. "He brought them out of darkness and the shadow of death, and broke their chains in pieces" (Psalm 107:14).

The kingdom of darkness has no hold on the person who makes praising God the practice of their life.

APPLICATION

WORSHIP:

As you begin to worship the Lord from the depths of your heart and sing praises to Him, I know beyond a shadow of a doubt that you will recognize that God's presence is with you and you will begin to feel the chains fall. Keep praising and see what God does as you adore Him and He surrounds you with His deliverance.

PRAYER:

"Jesus, I praise You. Even when it seems dark and circumstances do not look favorable, I sing to You because You are here with me. Your presence never leaves me. I am full of faith because Your presence and power are crushing the enemy and my chains are breaking into pieces. As I praise You continually, I trust in Your freeing power. I rejoice for change in my life and change in those around me as I praise. In Jesus' name I praise and pray. Amen."

DECLARATION:

"My chains of _____ are falling and I am set free as I praise my faithful God!"

ACTION:

Replace complaining and words of doubt with praise. Yes, it may seem illogical and does not feel good in the moment, but praise God. Praising God does not ignore the chains and dark circumstance you may be in, but it focuses on God who is much greater and is not intimidated by any impossibility. All things are possible with God and to him who believes. Praise is faith in God put into action. Praise today like never before.

DAY 38: MAGNIFY

I will bless the Lord at all times; His praise shall continually be in my mouth. My soul shall make its boast in the Lord; the humble shall hear of it and be glad. Oh, magnify the Lord with me, and let us exalt His name together. I sought the Lord, and He heard me, and delivered me from all my fears. They looked to Him and were radiant, and their faces were not ashamed. This poor man cried out, and the Lord heard him, and saved him out of all his troubles. The angel of the Lord encamps all around those who fear Him, and delivers them. Oh, taste and see that the Lord is good; blessed is the man who trusts in Him! (Psalm 34:1-8).

Praise is all about God, but since God inhabits praise and is present in the midst of praise, it powerfully frees you. We praise God for who He is and for His mighty works. True worship comes as we praise God for His glory and when we are sincerely grateful for all He has done.

Freedom is found as we praise, because two life-changing truths take place during praise. First and foremost, we see God as who He really is. Psalm 34:3 says to *magnify* the Lord. This word literally means "to show greatness." When God is magnified by praising Him, we are acknowledging and declaring the truth of God's greatness. Think for a moment about when you used a magnifying glass to look at something. This tool allowed you to see the details of something that you wouldn't be able to see without it. Magnifying the object does not make it bigger, but it looks larger to you because you are able to see the truth of what it is. When you praise God, you magnify Him because you are honoring who God is. God reveals His greatness, power, love, grace, and so many other attributes when you praise and magnify Him. You are able to see God clearly and closely; you see Him for who He really is.

The second life-changing truth is that we are transformed as we see God and know Him for who He really is. Not only do we see that the Lord is good, but we taste—or experience—His goodness (Psalm 34:8). The problems, hard circumstances, trials, and things we need freedom from come to pass. When we praise the Lord and we are focused on God's amazing nature, the things that seem too big to overcome become extremely small in size compared to God. Magnifying God causes you to see the truth of your problems. Your challenges in life are minimized as you magnify God. Sickness, financial challenges, emotional bondage, hard decisions, and hurtful people all become secondary to the amazing presence of God. This is where praising God frees you; the reality of God with you and for you causes you to overcome and live in victory (Romans 8:31, 37).

> Magnifying God causes you to see the truth of your problems. Your challenges in life are minimized as you magnify God.

Praise is all about loving God and giving Him all the glory and honor. The pure motive of praising God is not to receive anything, but to worship God for who He is and what He has done. But in God's graciousness, He blesses us as we magnify Him. God is honored during praise, but He gives back by giving us His presence. We come to God to adore Him and give Him glory, but as we see Him we are changed. Our praise to the Lord is part of surrendering and giving ourselves to Him, but no one can ever out-give God. As we give God praise, He gives back to us. As we magnify God, we receive freedom in His presence. God's presence can never be isolated or selfish, for when we come to rejoice in the Lord, we see Him and our faith in who He is and what He will do increases greatly. The testimony of David is amazing as he writes, "Oh, taste and see that the Lord is good" (Psalm 34:8).

What's your challenge? Your freedom is connected to praise. No matter what your challenge is, there is joy, freedom, peace, and victory in God's presence. Magnify God; taste and see that freedom is yours as you experience the beauty of God's presence in praise.

APPLICATION

WORSHIP:

Sing praises to God and be free as you see Him and experience Him.

PRAYER:

"Lord, I look to You. Forgive me for the times of not praising and magnifying You. I am sorry for seeing You as smaller than who You truly are. You alone are worthy of praise, and I thank You for Your goodness and grace. As I see You in praise and worship, may I find victory and freedom from anything in my life that is trying to keep me down. No one and nothing compares to Your goodness or great power. I praise You and trust You. In the name of Jesus. Amen."

DECLARATION:

"I will bless the Lord at all times; His praise shall continually be in my mouth" (Psalm 34:1).

ACTION:

See God's true nature as you lift up your voice to Him. Get lost in praise today. You will soon find that the challenges and attacks from the enemy will look small and powerless in God's presence.

DAY 39: THE GARMENT OF PRAISE

The Spirit of the Lord GOD *is* upon Me, because the Lord has anointed Me to preach good tidings to the poor; He has sent Me to heal the brokenhearted, to proclaim liberty to the captives, and the opening of the prison to *those who are* bound; to proclaim the acceptable year of the Lord, and the day of vengeance of our God; to comfort all who mourn, to console those who mourn in Zion, to give them beauty for ashes, the oil of joy for mourning, the garment of praise for the spirit of heaviness; that they may be called trees of righteousness, the planting of the Lord, that He may be glorified (Isaiah 61:1-3).

Praising God is a choice. You must decide to praise God; your feelings and circumstances may not always agree with the decision to praise God. Isaiah 61:3 is a prophecy of the ministry of Jesus, which He reveals about Himself in Luke 4:18. He goes on to say that He gives the "Garment of praise for the spirit of heaviness" (Isaiah 61:3). Praising the Lord is connected to the freedom, healing, and restoration that Jesus provides. The garment that He freely gives must be put on. When we put on the garment of praise, heaviness, depression, despair, and darkness flee. Again, God inhabits our praise, and when God's presence is realized and received when praise happens, darkness cannot remain in the presence of Light.

Jesus was anointed to preach the good news that heals the brokenhearted, brings liberty and freedom to the captives, opens prison doors for the oppressed, restores sight to the blind, and heals other physical diseases (Luke 4:18). He also exchanges your mourning with comfort and joy. He also exchanges days that are full of beauty and life in place of days of darkness and hopelessness. Jesus causes you to praise in exchange for despair, weakness, and defeat. Praise is like a garment; it is so much a part of your freedom that it rests on you. Praise wraps around you and covers you. Praise is what frees you, but it is also the result of freedom. In the natural you are always covered with a garment of clothing throughout the day. Likewise, you are to put on the garment of praise to God continually—before, during, and after you are liberated.

The garment of praise has been provided for you, but you must put on the garment. Since the garment of praise is to continually cover you, praise to the Lord is given in the hard times as well as the great times. God knew that you needed to be free from the enemies of darkness and despair, so that is why He calls you to put on the garment of praise. As you do, the spirit of heaviness flees. David played skillfully on his harp before the Lord for the sake of King Saul. When David played, the distressing spirit departed from Saul and he was refreshed and made well. God was with David and when he played unto the Lord, when David put on the garment of praise, Saul was refreshed in the presence of God (1 Samuel 16:14-23). The Lord is enthroned in the praises, so even those around us will experience the freedom and wonderful presence of God as we praise Him with our lips.

Sincere worship from the heart and praise from the lips will cast out the demonic forces that are so eager to destroy you.

Praise to the great I AM throws oppression out. Sickness and disease can't survive in the environment of praise. When the garment of praise is put on, depression and despair die. Sincere worship from the heart and praise from the lips will cast out the demonic forces that are so eager to destroy you. The power of the enemy is paralyzed when you praise. Fear and anxiety take a back seat in your life when you declare and sing about the goodness and faithfulness of God. Praise confuses the plans of the devil and releases the promises of God into your situation. The garment of praise heals, restores, and unlocks the shackles in your life, for God is with you and ready to act on behalf of your freedom.

Don't lay down your garment of praise, no matter what may tempt you to do so. Become a man or woman of praise. Wake up praising, work praising, exercise praising, drive praising, rest praising—*make your life a life of praise to the Lord.* Spend your days "Teaching and admonishing one another in psalms and hymns and spiritual songs, singing with grace in your hearts to the Lord" (Colossians 3:16). You will never regret wearing the garment of praise; it is full of freedom and life!

APPLICATION

WORSHIP:

Make praise the first garment you put on each day. Sing songs you know that connect you to God and glorify the Lord. Make a decision today to sing praises.

PRAYER:

"Jesus, I praise You and I lift my voice to You. In my times of doubt, fear, anxiety, frustration, and depression, help me to put on the garment You freely provide for me. I understand that my freedom is connected to my praise to You. I praise You with joy, thanksgiving, and expectation of You working in my life with love and power. In Jesus' name. Amen."

DECLARATION:

"I exchange my struggle of _____ for the garment of praise"

ACTION:

What do you feel like today? What has been a challenge? What garment are you wearing today? Instead of focusing on and empowering the darkness, make a decision to sing praises. Watch what happens in you when you put on the garment of praise. You will be different, look different, and will become comfortable with praise.

DAY 40: SHOUT!

So the people shouted when *the priests* blew the trumpets. And it happened when the people heard the sound of the trumpet, and the people shouted with a great shout, that the wall fell down flat. Then the people went up into the city, every man straight before him, and they took the city (Joshua 6:20).

When God's Word speaks of shouting to the Lord, it is referring to the raised voice of praise, victory, and triumph in battle. Shouting unto the Lord is not shouting like you may think of shouting today, in a negative connotation. When you shout from your mouth to God, it is a determined faith and assurance that God has given you what He has promised.

Shouting to God is full of emotion and comes from the depths of your spirit, where joy and gratitude are expressed in loud praise to God. Psalm 47:1 says, "Oh, clap your hands, all you peoples! Shout to God with the voice of triumph!" Shouting to God is confirming with your mouth that God is King, has all authority, and that you have the victory and freedom in Him.

In today's passage, God had just done the miraculous with Joshua and the children of Israel; they passed through the Jordan River onto dry ground. Joshua and the people were amazed at the faithfulness and power of God. Joshua was near the city of Jericho, and God called Joshua to lead the people to take the city and overcome it. The problem was that Jericho was a city secured with a giant wall protecting it. No one was able to penetrate the wall that wrapped around this great city, yet God promised that He would give them this city. Joshua needed to trust God regarding how He would give the city to them.

In Joshua chapter 6 (and I would suggest reading the whole chapter), the Lord instructed Joshua to take the Ark of the Covenant (God's presence), and march around the walls of the city of Jericho once each day for six days. On the seventh day, they were to march around the walls of Jericho seven times, and when they completed the seventh lap, the priests would blow the trumpets, and this would be followed by a shout unto the Lord. Joshua said, "Shout, for the Lord has given you the city!" (Joshua 6:16). When the priests blew the trumpets, it says, "And it happened when the people heard the sound of the trumpet, and the people shouted with a great shout, that the wall fell down flat" (Joshua 6:20). The enemy's defeat happened when God took down their walls. God used the shout of His people, or the battle cry of victory, to destroy the walls that were blocking their victory.

Your freedom comes through praise, and shouting to the Lord is the extreme outward manifestation of praise.

What walls have you wanted to see crash to the ground and be utterly destroyed? What has been keeping you from victory and freedom? What is in your way? The walls of greed and poverty keep you from financial freedom. The walls of anger keep you from the freedom of healthy relationships and peace. The walls of lust keep you from the freedom of purity and experiencing true love. The walls of depression keep you from the freedom of joy. The walls of fear keep you from walking in the purpose and will of God. The walls of unbelief keep you from the freedom of experiencing what God has promised to you.

Praising the Lord by giving a shout of victory will free you, and will knock the walls down. Walls may be intimidating to you, but not to God. Freedom is the will of God for your life. Jesus has provided all that you need to be free. Joshua and the children of Israel shouted to the Lord *before* the walls came down. Your freedom comes through praise, and shouting to the Lord is the extreme outward manifestation of praise. When you shout to God in faith, you cause the kingdom of darkness to shake and tumble down to defeat.

As you read the Word, think on the promises of God, declare His promises out of your mouth, apply the blood of Jesus, believe fully in God's love and power, follow what God commands, pray to the Lord, and praise Him like never before, you will certainly shout to God because you have been set free! Give God a shout of praise!

APPLICATION

WORSHIP:

Find a place where you will not scare or distract anyone, but praise the Lord by giving a shout. As you shout to God, know that you are free and the victory is yours. Shout with thanksgiving and amazement toward a wonderful God!

PRAYER:

"Lord, thank You for freeing me. I shout to You with a voice of triumph, not defeat. I thank You that the devil flees as I shout Your awesome name and shout my praise to You. I see the walls fall as I shout a battle cry of victory. As I have been freed, help me to continually walk and practice what You have taught me in Your Word so I can grow stronger and help others who need to be free. I trust You and pray this in the name of Jesus. Amen."

DECLARATION:

"I shout to God with a voice of triumph!" (Psalm 47:1).

ACTION:

Praise is not quiet. There is a place in prayer to be still to hear God's voice, but there is certainly a time to shout and sing praises loud to God. Your freedom is connected to shouting unto the Lord. Whatever wall needs to come down in your life, shout to God, knowing that God has delivered you. As you shout a battle cry of victory to the Lord, you are speaking in faith that the war has already been won. Don't be shy; shout unto the Lord and let His joy fill your heart.

CONCLUSION

It is my prayer that during the last forty days, God has transitioned you into wonderful transformation! God wants you to be free. I encourage and challenge you not to go back to the enslavement that once ruled your life (Galatians 5:1). If you haven't found complete freedom in a particular area of your life, do not be discouraged. You are still walking in the process of freedom through the keys found in God's Word. Do not accept Satan's condemnation, but rejoice that you are moving forward and have won more battles than before. Jesus has promised to complete the work He began in you (Philippians 1:6)!

What is important is that you make a daily decision to pick up the keys that God has already provided for you to use for your freedom. As you *read* (abide in the Word of God), *think* (meditate on the Word of God), *speak* (declare the Word of God), *apply* (receive the blood of Jesus), *believe* (put your faith in God), *obey* (follow God), *pray* (pursue God), and *praise* (rejoice in God), you will find that you will grow stronger in freedom. As you take the keys and apply them in your area of weakness and unlock the chains, you will truly be free!

Your freedom will be a testimony to multitudes of people who need the freedom you have experienced. May your children, your children's children, and many more find the freedom that comes through encountering Jesus and the truth of God's Word!

"Therefore if the Son makes you free, you are free
indeed" (John 8:36).

APPENDIX: THE BAPTISM IN THE HOLY SPIRIT

As discussed on Day 34, the baptism in the Holy Spirit is a necessary and vital gift that God commands every Christian to receive, graciously gives, and has promised to all believers (Acts 1:4-5). It is a separate work of the Holy Spirit from salvation. At salvation, the Holy Spirit comes to indwell within each believer (John 20:22; Ephesians 1:13-14). The baptism, or immersion, of the Holy Spirit takes place for the believer after salvation (Acts 2:1-4; 8:15-16; 19:1-6). The Holy Spirit comes to dwell in a believer at salvation; the Holy Spirit comes upon a believer for power to be a witness of Jesus Christ when baptized in the Holy Spirit.

The Holy Spirit at salvation benefits the one who believes and receives Christ. The Holy Spirit's role in the baptizing for empowerment is mainly for the benefit of the one being ministered to. In his book, *The Transformed Life*, John Carter explains the purpose of the baptism in the Holy Spirit:

> "Baptism in the Holy Spirit is a gift that infuses spiritual power into the life of the believer, enabling them to become effective witnesses. This power is a special anointing that produces a heightened sensitivity to the Spirit's presence, a greater operation of spiritual gifts through the believer, and a deeper hunger for spiritual things and insight into the Word of God. It also introduces the believer to a new dimension of worship and prayer."[1]

---

1. John Carter, *The Transformed Life* (2013, Harrison House Publishers: Tulsa OK), 142.

The Word of God graciously confirms what the initial sign is of being baptized in the Holy Spirit so that there is no guessing involved. The first, physical sign is speaking in tongues. Jesus said that one of the signs following those who have believed in Christ for salvation is that "they will speak with new tongues" (Mark 16:17). When the believers in the upper room were baptized, or filled, with the Holy Spirit, they spoke in other tongues (Acts 2:4). They had been waiting for the promise of the Holy Spirit as Jesus had commanded, which was the baptism in the Holy Spirit, and the evidence initially was tongues. It is a language that one does not know nor has ever learned, but is given by the Holy Spirit when baptized in the Holy Spirit. This language is given to declare from the mouth and is the language of prayer and worship that comes directly from the born-again spirit (1 Corinthians 14:14). This prayer and worship that comes from our spirit and released from our mouth is the perfect will of God because the Holy Spirit gives the utterance of what is said.

The Holy Spirit is not asking you to wait for Him to baptize you; He is waiting for you to ask to be baptized, filled, and immersed in this wonderful, life-changing experience.

It's amazing that God not only empowers us to witness and serve others through the baptism in the Holy Spirit, but continues to bless us and others by giving us the gift of tongues. Through speaking in tongues, we intercede on the behalf of others (Romans 8:16-17), we build up and edify ourselves (1 Corinthians 14:4), we worship our God (1 Corinthians 14:18), and we become refreshed as we speak in tongues in God's presence (Isaiah 28:11-12).

The baptism in the Holy Spirit with the evidence of speaking in tongues is the common life for the Christian. The question is, have you been baptized in the Holy Spirit?

The baptism in the Holy Spirit is God's will for you, and He requires that you receive this work of the Holy Spirit by faith. The baptism in the

Holy Spirit is a gift from God, and He desires all of His children to receive it (Acts 2:39). The Holy Spirit is not asking you to wait for Him to baptize you; He is waiting for you to ask to be baptized, filled, and immersed in this wonderful, life-changing experience (Luke 11:13).

MY STORY OF BAPTISM IN THE HOLY SPIRIT

I was saved when I was in high school; it was the first time I ever heard about being born again and that Jesus actually required it and talked about it for salvation. When I accepted Jesus into my life, I was part of a Pentecostal church. Consequently, I began to learn and understand what it means to be baptized in the Holy Spirit. I began to read and study about it in God's Word and I found out that it was a normal part of the early church, that the apostle Paul talked much about it in his letters, and that men and women in my church and churches around the world were still experiencing this wonderful promise.

I understood that it was God's will for every Christian to receive the baptism in the Holy Spirit, so I wanted to be filled to have power for being a witness and to pray in tongues. So I sought after it and asked God to fill me. I went to the altar many times to have pastors and guest preachers lay hands on me. Nothing happened. I began to wonder if it really was for me or if there was something I was doing wrong. It became discouraging, confusing, and frustrating. I didn't understand.

One night I was in my bedroom getting ready to go to bed. It was a summer night so I had my window open, and I was praying before laying my head down to fall asleep, as I often did. I remember asking the Lord why I wasn't baptized in the Holy Spirit with the evidence of speaking in tongues. In the still, quiet, yet powerful voice, the Holy Spirit showed me something about it. He said, "Sit up, ask Me to fill you, believe that I will, receive my filling as you surrender to the Lord, and begin to speak after you have asked for My baptism." I said to myself, "The Word says it, the Holy Spirit still baptizes and gives the utterance to speak in tongues, so I will ask, simply believe, receive because God promised it, and I will speak."

I sat up in bed and began to worship the Lord. Out of a heart of surrender, thanksgiving, humility, and obedience to God, I simply asked in faith for the Holy Spirit to baptize me and fill me. I was conscious of the presence of God as I adored Him and asked to be filled, and I began to open my mouth with sounds and a language that the Holy Spirit gave to me. The Holy Spirit did not possess my mouth and control it; I opened it and I spoke with my mouth. The tongues, or language, was given by the Holy Spirit, but I physically spoke out a sound that was, in fact, a supernatural utterance because only the Holy Spirit knew what I was speaking. Then I raised my hands and continued to speak in tongues, being filled with the Holy Spirit. It was childlike faith receiving and accepting what God had promised.

> ## Everyone's experience is different when being baptized in the Holy Spirit. It is wonderful, much like each person has a different testimony of salvation.

Everyone's experience is different when being baptized in the Holy Spirit. It is wonderful, much like each person has a different testimony of salvation. What is the same with everyone are the ingredients of knowing, believing, receiving, and acting by faith. I didn't have any outward manifestation other than speaking in a different language. It was matter-of-fact because God is powerful, yet very practical.

I am so blessed to have received the promise of the Holy Spirit. To this day, I love being empowered by the Holy Spirit to glorify Jesus and I love to sing and pray in tongues!

ASK

Pray a prayer similar to this:

> *"Lord, thank You for saving me. You have made me righteous and not guilty before You because of the blood*

of Jesus that has made me a new creation! Thank You for the Holy Spirit in me! As I have received Jesus by faith through grace, I now ask You, Jesus, to baptize me with the Holy Spirit. I receive the promise of the baptism of the Holy Spirit by faith through grace!

I believe that I receive. Fill me, Holy Spirit, and set me aflame with power to be a witness of Jesus Christ and to serve the body of Christ in power!" (Acts 1:8).

BELIEVE AND RECEIVE

Now begin to thank Him and praise the Lord with your mouth. Be genuine from your heart but vocal from your mouth! As you worship and praise, believing you are receiving the baptism, or infilling of the Holy Spirit, begin to use your mouth to speak the language the Holy Spirit is giving to you. Remember, the Holy Spirit does not control your mouth or move your lips. What you speak will not sound like a familiar language, but it is the language the Holy Spirit is giving you. It will sound different and it may not seem practical or understandable, but it is from God. As you speak it, the Holy Spirit will give the utterance. Continue to speak and receive the fullness of the Holy Spirit coming upon you, filling you, and empowering you. Praise and speak boldly in the language He has graciously given to you.

Walk daily in the Holy Spirit. Be empowered to share Jesus to a lost world. Pray and worship in tongues. Enjoy the freedom that comes from being baptized in the Holy Spirit!

ABOUT THE AUTHOR

Matt Muscatell is a passionate communicator of the Word of God. His desire is for individuals to encounter freedom by encountering Jesus and to experience the truth of God's word on a daily basis. Matt graduated from Valley Forge Christian College, located in Phoenixville, Pennsylvania. He has served in the ministry since 1996, seeing God's love and power setting multitudes free. He and his wife, Karen, have been married for twenty-four years and have two sons, Caleb and Noah. For more information on Matt, visit www.encounterfreedom.net

CPSIA information can be obtained
at www.ICGtesting.com
Printed in the USA
BVHW042105140221
600128BV00001B/2